AUTHORITY

How to Write Your Book and Use It as a Marketing Tool

MICHELLE WATSON

Breakfree Forever Publishing

Disclaimer

Author: Michelle Watson Title: AUTHORITY – How to Write Your Book and Use It as a Marketing Tool.

ISBN: 978-1999620141

Category: SELF-HELP/Marketing/Business: Breakfree Forever Publishing.

"Only you can determine
what is going to be written in the next chapter
of your book called life"

~ Michelle Watson

TABLE OF CONTENTS

DEDICATION

I am dedicating this book to my beautiful children Santana, Antonio and Alisha, my husband Allain and my grandparents Shilo, Ashley, Hazel and May. The many individuals who have taken the step to defeat all odds and create the life that they desire as well as those who are now helping society by sharing their stories so that others can learn from their journey.

FOREWORD

Since meeting Michelle, she has done a phenomenal job of not only starting her business but truly using her knowledge learnt to expand, inspire and impact lives. She not only shares her powerful story to make a difference but also shows individuals how to let their voices be heard through writing and guide them on how to also use  the book as a marketing tool for their business. There are plenty of books and courses about writing, however most of them speak more about the grammar, editing and the basic tasks about book writing but not share the guidelines or the know-how of making the content effective for you as an entrepreneur to be seen as the go-to expert and get in front of your target audience.

 Michelle has truly mastered the art of helping entrepreneurs to have a successful journey of writing, publishing and marketing their book whilst getting visibility and being positioned as an authority for their business.

Maybe you bought this book because you are interested in getting your business more publicity, credibility or have always desired to leave a legacy behind in the form of writing your book, whatever it is, Michelle has provided the tools and strategies for getting your content out of your head and into the hands of your ideal clients

This awesome book is filled with resourceful information and Michelle has given her all to ensure that you do not make the same mistakes as she did at the beginning of her book-writing journey. I have always been impressed with the way that she refuses to allow the hurdles that may have knocked her down to keep her down but instead rises to every occasion. This indeed is the passion behind all that she does to assist you in achieving great success. If you have already started your book journey or if it is merely a thought, I would recommend that you read this book as I am sure you will find all the answers to the many unanswered questions you may have.

So, Michelle, I congratulate you on accomplishing another huge step on the road to greater success and I would also like to take this opportunity to say a massive well done in helping others to leave their mark here on earth.

I wish even greater success ahead for you on your many ventures.

Andy Harrington
Sunday Times Best Selling Author
CEO Jet Set Speaker Ltd

INTRODUCTION

Some of the greatest challenges organisations, business starters or entrepreneurs face is having visibility, effective branding and securing a constant flow of customers in order to keep their business growing and many have spent a large sum of money in trying to get this right. However, once the right tools and strategies have been implemented then your business will be streamlining its way to success.

In today's society, more individuals are understanding the power of becoming an author, the authority that it gives them and the realisation that it is a powerful marketing tool, surprisingly though there is still a large quantity who are still unaware of the possibilities that can arise from becoming an author. There are a recorded 200 million registered businesses in the world and currently only 2.2 million authors, so just imagine the knowledge and potential that is still going unknown or missing. It is a proven fact that 80% of business starters struggle to get clients because they have not positioned themselves as an expert or the 'go-to person in their field' whilst others only get to one level in their business without the potential of further growth because they do not know how to monetise their content and offer more products and services after the entry point for their customers. As an established business owner or newcomer to the business world, you want to ensure that you have the positioning, credibility and authority that will ensure you are sought after instead of you doing all the chasing, this tends to lead to weariness, which may result in you also giving up. I am not saying that you will not have to put the work in before this is possible or that you shouldn't continue marketing even when you become sought after, but I am saying there needs to come a point where you are not constantly the head hunter but instead get head hunted also. This may sound familiar to you or someone you know might possibly be experiencing this right now, so I am sure you would agree with me that in order to see different results you need to implement a new strategy.

You may be asking how can a book help me or my business? On the other hand, how many books can I sell to further boost my income? Despite the misconception that you need to sell as many books as you possibly can in order to get rich, there are a number of indirect benefits to writing a book as a business author. If you are looking to make money directly from your book, then of course you are looking to write a bestselling book such as '50 Shades of Grey' or you are J.K.Rowling. The benefits of writing a book are more indirect - for example, establishing yourself as an expert in your field, thereby establishing your credibility and secondly, for the purpose of lead generation, getting prospects to show their interest by either purchasing or downloading as part of your marketing strategy. In addition, being approached for better speaking engagements to promote yourself and your business.

I have definitely seen those outcomes in my own business, and that of friends and colleagues who have also written books, and this is the purpose of this book; to show you the power in becoming an author, financially and even more important personally, as this will indeed be a legacy that will be left behind. Magazines, newspapers and fliers tend to fade away, but a copy of your book will always be available many years down the line. Now when you stop and think about it, is it then not a wise investment to promote your knowledge, expertise and content by using a book?

The next question you may be asking is, 'if this is so great a tool then why aren't more people doing it?' Here's the thing; many people are of the belief that to write a book it needs to be hundreds of thousands of words long, that their grammar needs to be perfect, or that they have to be highly educated, all of which are not true. You don't even have to speak a specific language - all of this can be outsourced, hence why there are editors, transcribers, translators etc.

The other issue is that people start to write and then you hear the statement 'I've got writers block' - have you ever heard that phrase? Maybe even you have made that statement and as a result, the book never gets finished. I have heard this so many times yet I want you to picture this – you or someone that you love dearly is held at gunpoint and the only way to be free is for you to complete the writing of your book - would you still have 'writers block?' or would you write even if it all didn't come out right? The fact is your 'why' wasn't strong enough to get it done. I want you to stop and think for a moment. If you were to apply the same level of importance of the 'why' or 'urgency' you need to accomplish the task as when held at gunpoint, then success would be assured, this is also one of the areas which will be covered in this book.

Another excuse is 'I don't know it all'; my question to you is, 'who said you needed to know it all?'. The moment you know it all is the day you stop learning. You don't have to know it all, as there are other professionals out there who have already figured out some of what you need to share, that extra information you may not yet know. You can do research or even interview them; I will share more about this later in the book.

In regards to not writing because there will be too many grammatical errors or that you are worried about spelling or that your language is not the best, I always remember this statement that I once heard, 'get it down then get it right' or even better, 'you cannot edit a blank page' so it doesn't have to be perfect, as this thought tends to be one of the most common beliefs that delays or freezes individuals to stagnancy.

I call perfectionism a 'permanent pause' as this is exactly what it does; it permanently puts you on pause making you fall victim to unproductivity despite having the knowledge, skills, ability and know-how.

In this book – Authority - I cover the many tips, strategies, and guidelines that will help you to get the content from within you to having a published book in your hand and better still, how to then use that book to create or increase your business.

You may have gone through many challenges, hurdles, made many mistakes and may even feel ashamed to share your story, but I want you to take the spotlight off yourself and think more about the lives that you can make a difference to by sharing your experiences; someone is waiting for your message. You cannot go back and rip out the pages in your life that have already passed but you have the ability to decide what will be written in your next chapter and the lives that you will help; the choice is yours to continue allowing others to write your book of life or to write your own.

Scan to connect with me on Social Media

www.break-freeforever.com

www.facebook.com/groups/
theauthorlounge/

bit.ly/MWYoutubechannel

CHAPTER ONE

The Power of Becoming an Author

"The past cannot be changed but the future is in your power."

~ Unknown

Have you ever strongly had the desire to achieve something but was just not sure how to and so it has left you in a place of stagnancy?

Maybe as you are reading this book you are thinking of giving up on your dream, purpose, career, business or even your life because of the many challenges, hurdles or roadblocks that you have gone through and are maybe still experiencing. Possibly, you no longer believe in yourself or capabilities as you have started on the road of entrepreneurship but just cannot seem to make it work. The bills are stacking up, you have become so stressed that your health is deteriorating and relationships crumbling. Maybe you are feeling so irrelevant due to the fact that you are constantly working, earning just enough to cover the bills, leaving no quality time for your family and the legacy that you have dreamt of leaving behind no longer seems possible. Maybe you own a small business or have just started out as an entrepreneur, but you are struggling to gain visibility and the ability to position yourself in front of your ideal clients. Potentially you could be getting more paying clients because you are truly an expert at what you do, but if only you knew how to get your content out there and have the ability to position yourself as the expert so that your clients would actually start chasing you rather than you burning the midnight oil every night trying to get their attention. Perhaps you want to upscale your business and stand out from amongst the usual noise of the marketplace, to be unique, different and be seen as an authority in your field. Maybe you are finding it difficult to maintain a balance between family life and the business, because you are the business and that freedom that you thought you were going to have when you left your J.O.B (Just Over Broke) position has slipped away. Maybe that's only a part of it, as the worse bit is that through all this you are not truly living the life that you desire as you have settled for second best, doing daily tasks or the job that you hate and living your life for others - which really means that YOU, the real you, has died.

However, I want you to imagine – imagine that you are now living your desired dream, the debts are cleared, and you are financially free and able to take your family on holidays when and where you like. Imagine that now you are no longer stuck in that dead-end job but running a successful business. Imagine positioning yourself to be seen as the expert in your field, you now have an increase in clients who are actively looking for you because you now have visibility, which then also means an increase in your income and the growth of your business. You have time for the family as you are now enjoying multiple streams of residual income and you earn money whilst you sleep. You are now making a difference and are on the path of leaving a legacy behind.

Have you ever had a time in your life when you wondered to yourself how much more you would be able to achieve if you knew exactly how to action whatever it is that you are doing or want to accomplish right from the get-go? I know right, it would be absolutely phenomenal! Unfortunately though, life does not necessarily always work that way. The good news is that there is someone out there whether you believe it or not who has already gone through your current experience and could possibly save you two of the most important and valuable elements of life that I am sure matters to you, and that is TIME and MONEY. I was one of the many that had to go through some major roadblocks which I call the learning process, and I will share some of these lessons with you later; this is what will help to bridge the gap from where you are now to your desired destination - the position of becoming an AUTHORITY!

Possibly you are either an entrepreneur, business owner, someone who is interested in becoming an author and wants to publish your content in order to gain visibility and use it as a marketing tool to increase value, generate leads and get you on to various platforms that will enable you to grow.

You just might be asking the question – 'can a book really help me?' 'Is all this really important or worth it?' Well here's the thing; how important is your business, life and the legacy that you desire to leave behind? I want you to think about this fact – a book never dies, it remains forever, is something that will continue to be read and help others even after you have gone, it's a lifetime business card.

A very good example of this is the great Napoleon Hill. I am assuming you have never physically met him as he died in 1970 but yet his presence still lives on, as if you have. Why? Because you have met him through the work he has left behind, the majority of it being the books that he has written. One that truly caught my attention was 'Outwitting the Devil.' After the release of 'Think and Grow Rich', Hill began writing 'Outwitting the Devil' as an explanation of why some were still seeing failure after following all of the steps in 'Think and Grow Rich'. His wife, Annie Lou, did not want the book published because of the role the Devil played in it. When Hill died in 1970, the manuscript went into the possession of Annie Lou, who died in 1984. After her death, the manuscript went into the hands of Dr. Charles Johnson, who was Annie Lou's nephew and president of the Napoleon Hill Foundation. While Dr. Johnson believed the book's message to be powerful, his wife, Frankie Johnson, shared Annie Lou's feelings and told Dr. Johnson that she did not want the manuscript published while she was alive. After Frankie's death, Dr. Johnson passed the manuscript to Don Green, CEO of the Napoleon Hill Foundation. Sharon Lechter was then asked to edit the manuscript, and after several years of annotations and reviews, it was released in June 2011. Book Depository has stated that this book has sold over 27 million copies, hence still making a massive impact even to this day, not only to the reader but no doubt as well to the finances of The Napoleon Hill Foundation and his family, his lineage. Now that's what we call a true legacy.

I want you to now think of the later generation including your lineage knowing about you years after you have left this earth, learning about your challenges, accomplishments and solutions you have created in an ability to help others and them also, because the challenge you faced may just be one someone from your lineage will most likely also experience. Whether we like it or not we are all going to die one day, this is inevitable, but you can allow your memories to live on – remember, a book never dies.

AUTHORITY

Is it important and necessary to be seen as an authority in your field in order to make a significant difference in the life of others, my business and life?

Let us firstly take a look at some words that come from the Oxford English Dictionary of what authority means. Command, control, mastery, sovereignty, person in charge, verifiable, authentic, self-confident and respected. Most people tend to say that people of authority are demanding, a bully or someone who is constantly instructing others to do what they say. However, I believe that is not true, because I believe that a person of authority is a leader, someone who stands out, that leads from the front and leaves a path behind for others to follow, a trail blazer, someone positioned in order to leave a legacy behind.

In every arena of life, there is a follower and a leader. Someone has to set the pace, now does that make the individual a bully? I do know that some take advantage of their position. However, the truth is that authority is the position, but leadership is the character. Which one would you prefer to be, the leader in a position of authority or to constantly remain the follower? The chain of command that leads to one leaving a legacy behind requires the right positioned leaders and those leaders will indeed need followers. Everyone in some way is a follower as you will need a mentor in order for you to also grow, so that you can too become that authority figure and have followers. You may be wondering as to how it is that it's the person of authority who will become the strong legacy leaver?

Let us take a look for instance at President Obama. He entered into the position of authority and left a strong legacy behind as he became the first black President of the United States of America. If he remained a follower it would not be so; I don't know about you but for me, I didn't know anything about Barack Obama until he took the step to run for President, which immediately changed his position from being a follower to an authoritative figure. You becoming an author creates the platform for you to be in a position of authority in your field, to be a go to person and expert. Being in that position, your value automatically increases, and you are now seen as the person that others can follow. The moment President Obama entered into his position his value changed. This as well will happen for you once you become an author and use it wisely.

Another question you may be asking is, 'Ok, I get it that the book will enable me to leave a legacy behind but what can it do for me and my business right now?' Firstly, just as the title of this book states 'AUTHORITY' – there is power in the words 'I am an author', in fact the etymology of authority is 'author.' People start to take more notice of you and look at you with a totally different perspective, you are no longer looked at as a novice but as a figure with purpose and authority. This helps tremendously with your positioning in the marketplace, increasing visibility and allowing clients to find you. A unique status that will also enable you to increase your value and simultaneously your income, what you charge and the growth in your business. Another way that it will assist is by saving you money with your marketing, you make a one-off investment to write and publish your book and as I mentioned earlier, it is a lifetime business card. Imagine a potential high-end client asking you for a business card and you present them with your book; you have just stood out from the others who have merely handed in a business card no matter how classy the card may look. Think about how much money you may have already spent on marketing materials or the newspaper and magazine advertisements and that is only for a temporary period of time - all this and more I will be going into throughout the content of this book. Time is everything and what better time to start saving money and growing your business. However, if you have not yet started your business and you have been thinking about it, what are you waiting for? What better way to start out than as someone already in a place of authority.

There are various stages in life that I believe one needs to go through in order to truly leave a mark on this earth and create a successful and sustainable business and legacy. I want you to take a look at the diagram below and see if you can identify what stage you are currently at.

The **PROCRASTINATOR** is one that takes enough steps that will enable them to pay for their expenses and daily requirements. Despite taking limited action they remain in the comfort zone and are not interested in venturing beyond. They easily adapt a poverty mindset without even realising it and are possibly earning between the range of £0-20k. They are normally the ones that settle for second best instead of living their purpose, constantly putting things off, having the 'yes' attitude but limited action.

The **DABBLER** is someone who is never deeply engaged or involved in anything. They tend to take things lightly and are not seriously committed to their activities so almost everything they start is short-lived. You would see them five different times in the year and each time they would have told you about completely different ventures that they are doing each time. They are afraid to start or stay loyal enough to see anything through to the end and easily divert when a challenge arises – their 'WHY' is not strong enough and they may be earning between the range of £20k-£50k.

The status of **AUTHORITY** is being an influencer, leader, and a person whose real or apparent authority over others inspires or attracts attention; they are now in the position of visibility and sought after. This individual is constantly moving the bar and seeking ways to improve and increase their results. The authoritative figure leads through influence rather than demanding authority, which is the most important quality of a great leader. They have emotional intelligence, effective communication, negotiation and consensus building skills and carry a powerful presence wherever they go. They have mentors and peers that push them beyond their norm and leads them to the level that they desire to be, which might be where their mentors and/or peers are currently at. They are making marks on the earth whilst creating the pathway that is building a legacy to leave behind, and most likely running a sustainable business that has various entities, streamlining multiple avenues of residual income. The authoritative figure is earning between £50k-1 million and continuously invests and seeks ways to also create opportunities for others, as they have loyal followers and raving fans and this category is the minimum of where you should be aiming to be.

The **HIGH-ACHIEVER** is an action taker and generates great results. They are constantly moving their goal posts to obtain higher achievements and do not allow themselves to stay within the boundaries of a comfort zone. They are very far from a mediocre way of thinking and will always aim to be more than average, just good or satisfied with the status quo. High achievers are creative and always actively seeking for better, different or faster approaches to hit their goals, always aiming to improve or try new ways to do so. They are performance driven and leaders, just like the authority figure, they stay in circles that will challenge them to be and achieve more. This individual is a risk-taker who will do what it takes to move beyond the position they are in. A visionary, with a no-nonsense mentality when it comes to work, they are focused, disciplined and have a winning mentality; when knocked down, they get back up again. They are success orientated and fall in the £1 million - £10 million income bracket.

The **LEGACY-LEAVER** is someone who is unforgettable as an influential leader and they have gone through all the levels mentioned above and have a proven trail of success, a true overcomer and pacesetter and in the position to leave a bequest that can be handed down, endowed or conveyed to another.

This however is not only to their own lineage, but to the world. They are a predecessor who effectively leaves a legacy through transformation, value, vision, inspiration or wealth. They generate vast levels of income generally ranging from £10 million upwards. They are visible, sought after and hold a strong position in their circle. A legacy-leaver is passionate about their vision and tends to leave foundations behind to ensure that their mission continues long after they have left this earth, strong enough that they are continuously remembered. They have a large community of loyal followers or raving fans and have systemised their services or unique solution that it all runs without them, duplicating and leaving a trace of themselves all over the world.

The questions here now for you are; in which one of these categories do you currently fall? Where is it that you desire to be? Are you willing to do what it takes in order to get there?

WHY NOW?

Time is a very precious commodity and should be treated as such. So many times we say tomorrow but tomorrow never comes. I can bet you have been thinking about writing a book for a long time, but it just has not happened. Maybe because you are either saying 'I don't have the time' or saying 'I will do it at some point.' Both statements revolve around the time factor. I want to now ask you a very profound question. 'Have you ever insured your gadgets, phone, laptop etc or if you drive, your car maybe?' I am sure that you have, so that if anything goes wrong you can get it replaced; but where have you insured your time?

If you were not happy about how you spent your yesterday or if something went wrong, could you call an insurance company and tell them that you need a time replacement, or could you go to the store and say I bought myself some time? However, I don't like it so can I get a refund? It's just not possible. We say time is precious, but do we truly treat it as such. What results do you want to achieve tomorrow? Well here is the thing, your tomorrow starts from today.

A common statement that many tend to make is, 'I am dyslexic and not able to write a book.' 'I get writers block.' 'I don't have enough content to put inside a book,' and the list goes on and on. However, do you know what I think? I think all of that is absolute nonsense and this is with no apology. It's all just a way for you to talk yourself out of taking the step. The matter of time is just that you did not plan or put it into your focus.

I will share an example with you. I have been on a journey to lose weight for the past six years and have always yo-yoed as I would revert to old habits of eating. I always used the excuse that I didn't have the time to exercise or go to the gym but the truth was, it wasn't that I didn't have the time but instead that I didn't make time for it. Now what do I mean by this? Well in order for me to meet with a client, attend seminars or speak at events, I would have to plan, check my schedule and then slot it into the diary. However, when it came to exercise, I didn't do this, and do you know why? The same reason why you don't. For you, it might not be the exercise but something else that you have been procrastinating about, for instance, your book. It is the fact that you have not applied a high level of urgency, need or importance to it. It is the same for all the other excuses you tell yourself. I spoke about this in my other book, 'Rise Above and Believe – It's Do or Lie, How to Get Rid of Excuses and Create Your Desired Life'. I also mentioned in the introduction about the scenario where if someone precious to you was held at gunpoint until you completed the task, what would your excuse be? There would be none because you would have applied a level of urgency to it.

You may say Michelle, my issue is not time related but more to do with my lack of ability due to me having a learning difficulty such as dyslexia or other associated special need, so how is it possible? One way around it is to purchase a Dictaphone or even download a voice recorder App on your phone or device and then get a transcriber to type it up for you then an editor can then edit or proofread it for you. Another way is an example of a client of mine who was a professional boxer. He was dyslexic and did not want to use a voice recorder and so I offered him an additional service which was to interview him and write his manuscript based on the content that he was sharing. There is a saying which I always used to hear my grandmother say when I was growing up, 'where there is a will, there is a way.' The question is, not can I do it but instead, how badly do I want it?

Are you truly maximising your full potential and utilising your time here on earth or are you allowing yourself to remain stagnant by coming up with all the limiting excuses you can find in order to talk yourself out of it? The only cure to the illness of 'possibility blindness' which is telling yourself the many reasons why you cannot achieve your dreams, is to take action.

I heard a story once about a dog that all of a sudden kept whining and making painful howling noises and one night the neighbour of the owner could not sleep and decided to go and speak to the owner to find out what the problem was. On getting to the house he saw the dog sitting on the front porch but couldn't see what was causing the dog to sound as if it was in pain. The owner came out and so the neighbour asked "my dear neighbour, what is going on with your dog these past few days, his constant whining of pain is getting really annoying?" The owner replied casually "he is fine, he is just sitting on a nail." Astonished by the owners reply, the neighbour said, "so why doesn't he just get up off of it?" "Well" said the owner, "I guess it's because it is not painful enough."

Are you truly maximising your full potential and utilising your time here on earth

So, my question to you is, what nail are you sitting on that you have been whining about so much that even those around you are affected by it? Maybe it's your job, the lack of growth in your business, difficulty in getting clients or is it the fact that you have not yet started the business you have always said you were going to or maybe it is the book you haven't written. You know those ever-repeating new year's resolutions? You are living in the world of procrastination and that is the killer of all dreams. Whatever it is, it is obviously not painful enough for you to take a stand and remove yourself from it, just like the dog, you remain sitting on it and whining, waiting for someone to come and do it for you. Do not be the individual that I call 'the spoon-fed success achiever'

- you want to achieve but not do the work in order to get your desired results.

You may be asking, who is she to be talking to me about this and why does she think that she knows what she's talking about? Well I guess it's time for me to share my story with you.

HOW IT ALL BEGAN

My name is Michelle Watson. For those who do not already know me, I am a bestselling author, business book creation mentor, publisher, business creation coach, multi-award winning speaker, co-pastor, founder of Breakfree Forever Consultancy, Women Be and co-founder of M.E.N (Men Empowerment Network). However, more importantly, I am the mother of three beautiful children and a wife to one of the best men in the world. The question is how did this all become possible?

As detailed above, there are numerous positions that I hold as a business woman, but it did not come about easily. For a long time, I was lost, unsure of where my life would be and the purpose of me being here on this earth.

Have you ever been on a night out that turned into the morning after and as a result experienced a massive headache?

Well if you were with me in the year 2005 you would have seen me in this very position – only my headache was not from drinking. You would have seen me standing with my back against the locked door in my small magnolia painted bathroom. The white porcelain bath to my right, the toilet to the front on my left and the hand basin immediately in front of me below the window that I always thought was oversized for a bathroom. There was a distinct smell of bleach playing havoc on my nostrils, but that was because I always cleaned my bathroom with copious amounts of bleach.

'Oh no, is that him?' I jumped as I heard a sound and crouched sideways to put my ear close up to the door. I knew he wasn't gone and was still out there waiting for me to come out. Why was I here again? Over and over I told myself no more – it wasn't going to happen again but yet somehow I still ended up finding myself in the same or worse position. Nicky kept telling me, but I never listenened, "Michelle don't you see that he is going to kill you. Are you going to remain like this forever? You refuse to tell your family and all you do is get up and write in journals as if you can write it all away." Nicky is a close friend of mine; you know the ones that tell it like it is, with her hint of a Jamaican accent. She just didn't understand. I couldn't just leave and become a divorcee in my early twenties. How could someone that once looked at you with so much love and compassion now look at you with such hate? How could the hands that once made you tingle now make you feel pain? How could the smile that once made you melt now just curdle your blood, and the words that made your heart skip a beat now change to so much filth that you felt like the scum of the earth. He was like Dr. Jekyll and Mr. Hyde, you know the character with two personalities, and to be going through this with him for five years had slowly destroyed me. The shame of telling my family was too much, to tell anyone was too much. Nicky only knew because she had seen the marks and heard the sounds.

All I wanted was one night out with my friends. You see, I had just been told that I had a tumour behind my left ear, resting on my nerve, and there was a 99% chance that the left-side of my face would be paralysed after the operation. I just wanted to be with my friends, something that I had also been deprived of and as you can guess, he was not happy about that. So there I was with my head spinning like a butterfly and my bruises stinging like a bee as if I had just gone through a few rounds in the ring with the great Muhammad Ali.

Oh no, the kids! I had to get out, I couldn't let him take the kids.

Have you ever made a decision, a very big decision? Well that night I decided not to just face whatever was coming to me by stepping out of the bathroom, but I also stepped out of the marriage. I would love to tell you that it was easy, but it was not, as I found it hard to tell my family because I felt ashamed and spent most days staying at my friend's house.

Have you, have you ever played the board game Snakes and Ladders? You've shaken your dice and got the biggest numbers, two sixes, and you happily move up your spaces and oh boy, are you excited, because you end up also getting a bonus to climb higher by going up the ladder, only to land on the mouth of a snake which takes you all the way back down to his tail at the very beginning of the board?

Well four months later you would have seen me stepping into yet another small room. Brilliant white painted walls, sofa to my right, a desk and chair to my left and a massive plant standing in the corner. There was a lovely smell of summer breeze and the room was brightly lit but somehow, I seemed to have darkness all around me. There he was, tall, dark and handsome. He could have been a basketball player apart from the glasses perched on his nose that made him look a bit like a nerd. "Hello Michelle, do come in and take a seat. Is it alright for me to call you Michelle?" He said with his bright but yet soft spoken voice. "Yes," I replied, hardly able to open my mouth. "I prefer to stand if that's okay" "Yes Michelle, whatever makes you comfortable. So I have gone through your notes and forms that you have completed, but can I hear from you what really brings you here today?"

My hands began to shake and the erratic, cracked voice that began to speak sounded nothing like me. "I feel like I am going mad and I know they think I am going mad, but I know he is following me." "Michelle, who is following you?" "My ex. He is following me wherever I go. I will go to the store and he's there; I leave my house to go to work and when I return, all of my clothes were missing from the closet. Another time it was my purse and passport. I go to my friend's house and all four of my car tyres get slashed outside her house; that's not a coincidence. Every morning when I get up, my car has another key mark on it. I have gone to my bed and woken up to find him standing over me. No one seems to be able to help. The police say that because he lived there his fingerprints would be all over the house anyway and unless they had proof, they could not prevent him from

34

coming to the house. I am too ashamed to tell my family all that's happening. I can't eat, sleep or even take care of the children properly, I can't take it anymore, I just can't take it anymore!" The tears flowing along with what little strength I had left.

"Michelle, it is ok, but is that the reason why you attempted to kill yourself?"

"I just want the pain to stop, I know it was wrong. How could I do this to my beautiful children? Who would have been there for them, my beautiful Santana, when it's time for her prom or Rashaun, my sweet boy who has special needs you know, who would be there to help him? How could I do this, how could I do this? I just want it all to stop."

"It will Michelle, it will, as you did the right thing by getting in touch. I always say to my clients that no one can answer a phone call that hasn't been made. You have made the call and we are here to help you. You are stronger than you know. I read through your notes and realised that whilst dealing with all this you recently had an operation to have a tumour removed; I assume all went well?" I replied with a nod of the head. "Michelle, it's not too late to turn your life around, and with the right help, you will be fine. You will be there to look after your children, but in order to do that you have to first take care of you. I can see from your notes here that one of your favourite hobbies is writing, well guess what, you have the ability to rewrite your history and turn things around, you just have to allow us to help you."

Rewrite my history…. what was it that Nicky had asked me again? Oh yes, did I think it was possible to write it all away? Here he was telling me that I did have the ability to rewrite my history.

Have you ever had a time in your life when you wished that your life was actually a physical book where you could go back, rip out the pages of the things in the past you did not like or wasn't happy with, perhaps with regards to an ex-partner or a costly mistake that you made? Unfortunately, that's not possible, but I realised at that moment that I may not be able to rip out the pages of my past but that I could make a difference to my future and so with the help of the councillor, my church and family, you would have seen me stepping into my power. You would have seen me on a spiritual journey whilst also working on myself through personal development.

> I may not be able to rip out the pages of my past but that I could make a difference to my future

I started reading self-development books like Dale Carnegie, "How to win Friends and Influence People," Robin Sharma, "The Saint, The Surfer and the CEO," Joyce Meyer, "Battlefield of the Mind," and Willie Jolley, "A Setback is a Setup for a Comeback." I started to listen to powerful people like Les Brown, Lisa Nichols, Tony Robbins, and Jim Rohn. You would have seen me on a spiritual journey as well as attending seminars such as MasterCoach, and The Coaching Academy at which I achieved my accreditation as a life coach, Mpowerment Ltd, where I learnt NLP (Neuro Linguistic Programming), and you would have seen me finding out who Michelle truly was. I then decided that I wanted to help people as well, just like how the councillor, my pastor and the personal development world had helped me, and so I signed up to a programme to write my story so I could share it and help others, even if only one person ever read it.

There were some critical and negative people along the way, you know the sort, those people known as the 'naysayers.' "So what qualifies you to write a book?" "Will anybody buy your book when they don't even know you?" "You went through depression and attempted suicide; how can you be qualified to write a book in order to help others – are you for real?" "So, you are J.K. Rowling now, huh?" However, I decided that even if the book just helped me to get everything out there, then that would be enough. Nevertheless, people were coming up to me slowly but surely and saying, "Wow, your story is amazing." "You need to share this story, it really helped and inspired me." This was all great, but I had used up the last of my savings to write the book, and now that I had, and I was inspiring others with my story, there was no money coming in and the business that I had in mind seemed terribly far away.

I then joined Andy Harrington's Professional Speakers Academy. I didn't have the money at the time, but I decided that I was going to make it happen somehow and went home to pull out all the gadgets, clothes and shoes I had that were just sitting there and I sold them. My now new husband, Allain, thought I was mad, but I told myself that when I made my money, I could always buy them back again.

I had now learned that I needed to get my message out to more people, not just one-on-one, not just one person reading my book, but to share the message of hope and help to as many people who, just like me, had got dealt a bad card, and that's why I decided to take action because I wanted to help those who had been on that road just like me, but the question was, how? The book, even though becoming a bestseller, wasn't doing anything. I had started my business on the side as a certified life coach, but that was not moving. I was going from one mentorship programme to the next, attending seminars, getting psyched up, returning home and finding myself back to square one as I had no idea what to do. It became frustrating as I kept meeting other authors like myself that had also written a book. They were unknown, and I kept hearing the common story of how they had spent a lot of money writing their book or starting their business but then that was it.

I remember one Friday attending a session of Andy's Professional Speakers Academy quarterly meetings in 2017 at the Thistle Hotel, Heathrow, and Andy was on stage, looking smart as usual with his white shirt neatly tucked into his trousers and despite his short stature, he always had a large presence when on stage. I remember looking at him and thinking to myself, 'so how is it that I think this small man is going to help me solve my big problems?'

"So, here's the thing. In life, you can either be the problem or you can be the solution, all you have to do is figure out what problem you can solve, package it and sell it. You break it into three levels: DIY (do it yourself), DWY (do it with you) or DFY (do it for you)."

That immediately sent bells ringing in my ear, and at that moment I wrote down all the challenges I was currently facing and decided to see how I could solve them. I then wrote my second book 'Rise Above and Believe.' I wrote, edited, designed the layout, in fact the full works and published it within ninety days. This book was written based on my 'unique branding solution' that I had created at PSA for my coaching business.

I then decided to use it as a business tool and see how I could use it to drum up business. I sent a copy to Her Majesty the Queen and got a letter of commendation in return. I did media releases and started to get TV and radio interviews. I was getting asked to speak at more events which then inspired me to create my own events, the first one being 'Women Be,' - a women's empowerment and networking event, and by using Andy's system, I was able to create my business and generate multiple streams of income.

I created a programme to help business owners and entrepreneurs write their business book and use it as a marketing tool as I had successfully done for myself. I started helping individuals that had ideas but didn't know how to turn them into a monetised business. I have won numerous awards such as Andy Harrington's Professional Speaker Academy ACE Mentor of the Year, multiple speaker awards, a performance coach of the year award, an empowerment woman of the year award, to name but a few. I have mentored and helped people ranging from business owners to professional boxers and singers, published numerous

> You don't have to be great in order to start but you do need to take a step in order to achieve your greatness

authors who have also become bestsellers and award winners, including my seven year old daughter, Alisha. I am truly fulfilling my purpose and leaving my mark on this earth so those to come will know that I was here.

I have learnt some very valuable lessons on this journey, which I will share with you. The first one being that success does not define you but instead you define success. The second is that you don't have to be great in order to start but you do need to take a step in order to achieve your greatness, and the third but most powerful for me is that you might not be able to go back and rip out the pages of your past that you are not happy about, but you do have the power to determine what will be written in the next chapter of your book called 'life'.

Watch me deliver this story to an audience in Amsterdam

youtu.be/n3EojyaNySk

CHAPTER TWO

The Primary Objective

Great, so now you have heard about me and how I used my book as a marketing tool and became a business book creation mentor and publisher, so now let me share with you the system I created in order for you to be able to do the same.

This system is unique, in the fact that it was created by me and cannot be found elsewhere. In my experience I have come to realise that there are five key elements that will help you to have true success with the creation and publication of your business book. The first being your 'primary objective.' This is not the first point by mistake because I believe that it is very crucial and also a significant first step for you to take on this journey in order to successfully get to your destination. By having a primary objective, you will be able to have clarity on the direction that you are going with your book, and have a clear understanding of who your target population is and how to make a memorable impact with your book. The importance of the primary objective, (which I call P.O,) is that you don't just start the journey, but that you make it to the end. As you can imagine, it's one thing to start writing your book, but it is another story to complete it. Having a P.O ensures that the content you share will be relevant to your readers and drives your potential clients to you. During the writing stage, at all times, it will help you to keep the end result in mind, which is to use the book as a marketing tool.

One of my mentors, Andy Harrington, always makes an honest statement about himself that makes people laugh, "If my lips are moving, I am selling." However, the beauty with him is that unlike others who would make that statement, he actually delivers quality content that truly helps and yields exceptional results for his clients, so he has no reason to feel ashamed making that statement. Why am I referring to this? Well here is the thing. When you are writing a business book it is completely different from a passion book (which is something I will explain shortly), so the moment that your pen is writing or your keyboard is tapping, you should be selling, but just like I stated about Andy delivering valuable content, you should be ensuring that the quality you deliver is relevant, helpful and informative enough for you to be seen as the 'go to person' and expert in your field but at the same time incomplete so that they will want more. Having your P.O will help you with just that. However, without it, you will be at a loss; the task will become more difficult and longer than necessary. You may write information that is not relevant to your target market and end up displacing yourself and lose focus along the way without completing your book. I am sure that some of you that are reading right now may possibly have started writing your book years ago but have never finished it.

PASSION BOOK VS. BUSINESS BOOK

You may be asking, 'what is the difference between a passion book and a business book?' It is almost the same as saying 'what is the difference between fiction and non-fiction' or 'the difference between passion and profit?' A passion book is more related to your story or pain that you have faced or someone else has, that you are passionate about and does not necessarily have to be literature that is factual but can be created even from imagination in order to address an issue related to your passion. Yes, a passion book can also be factual as most people tend to write their stories or someone else's. It's normally more difficult to argue as it has the possibility to be less factual or referenced. You may argue and say that a passion book can still be a good earner and get you visibility and yes, you would be right, but it would not completely address the purpose of your business book. For example, two men are in possession of the same car, having the same model, colour, specification etc. One of the men is just coming to give you a lift, the other is a car salesman, and he is coming with the intention to sell you the car. Which one do you think is most likely to go more in depth about the car and which one will go into more detail around it - the salesman or the one giving you a lift? You see they both have different purposes and that determines the outcome of their visit. The one that is giving you a lift may just be doing it as an errand, as a friend or has passion for driving, so even though he may know a lot about the car and driving, he's not selling it to you so you cannot buy it. The thing is, your client cannot buy what you are not selling. However, the salesman's sole purpose is to make a sale by showing you all that the car can do, so he is not just going to give you a drive but go into full details that will help you make your decision to buy and that is the major difference between the two.

The purpose of your business book is indeed what it says on the tin; to enhance your business and be a sales rep in order for your reader to know you, to see what it is that you have to offer, your content and how working with you will benefit them and finally to assist in making the sale. When writing your business book, you have to keep that in mind. Another point is that when writing your passion book, you are writing with yourself in mind, whereas with your business book, at all times, you need to have your ideal client or avatar in mind. I will speak more about this when we get to figuring out your target audience.

A business book, unlike a passion book, requires the need to give more references and quotes to the story or information; this is needed to ensure your content is more credible. Once you have made the decision on what sort of book you are writing, it will enable you to have a clear idea of who you are serving or how it will be beneficial for your clients and business.

Is it possible to combine both? Well firstly, it depends on if what you are doing for your business is your passion and secondly, if you can ensure that you don't lose sight of the end goal, which is to use it as a marketing tool. I have combined both when writing this book as it is addressing what I am passionate about; writing and helping others to share their story. I also shared my story in chapter one, which is a good way of you sharing about you, who you are, what it is that you are passionate about, and what you stand for but at the same time keeping the purpose in sight. The next question you may have is, 'which one do I do first?' My response is based on my experience and that of my clients, which is to do the business book first and get established as the authority as the business book will obviously bring more profit and provide the finance to produce the passion book. The main thing is that you obviously prioritise, based on your own needs and circumstances. I would, however, advise that you do the business book first. If you are saying that for you, it is not about your clients, business or money, then definitely the business book is not for you.

Ok. Now that you have clarified which book you are writing, it is time to concentrate more on the primary objective. I mentioned to you earlier what will happen if you take the time to figure out your P.O and what will happen if you don't, so now let me tell you what it is and why it is important. A primary objective is like having a roadmap allowing you to know where you are, where you want to go, know how you are going to get there, the resources needed and the purpose of going. The mistake many people make when they go on a journey of writing a book is that they don't have or do what I call 'The W.R.I.T.E Authors Journey.' The first point will enable you to have a purpose for writing your book, which without, may end up with you writing aimlessly with no point or reasoning behind it. And what am I talking about? I am talking about having a '**WHY**' and what do I mean by why? Novice authors may lack objective or a reason for writing their book. The problem with that is it may cause you to have a lack of purpose or drive for the book and so you may end up paying a lot of money and spending a lot of energy in the beginning but not seeing it through to the end meaning loss of time, money and clients. Your 'WHY' should be big enough that when you feel like giving up, the why will keep you going. A big part of your why should be the people that you know your content will help. You also need to know exactly the reason why you want to write your book for your business. Your book can be used to raise your visibility, develop your authority, generate leads for your business, bring you more clients, get speaking opportunities, sell products, launch businesses, switch careers, and achieve many other objectives.

> **Your 'WHY' should be big enough that when you feel like giving up, the why will keep you going**

I have stated some of the most likely reasons that individuals write a business book. I would advise that you take the time to look at page 47 and clarify what may be your reason why you want to write the book before moving to the next stage. It is totally ok if you end up choosing more than one or even all of the reasons stated in the image. The big benefit of having a why for writing your book is that it will help you to write a book that will not be for self-development purposes, but instead bring benefits to you, the reader and your business; an effective marketing tool that gets the results that you require in order to boost your business.

In figuring out the why behind your book, you also need to clarify who your target population will be and to do this you need to ask yourself these questions.

- Who is my book for?
- Who is my ideal client?
- What gender are they?
- What is their age gap?
- What are their pains, needs and desires?
- Do I have the content to provide them with their solution?
- Is there a need for your book and what is it?

These questions will indeed enable you to help figure out if the book will be congruent with your business clients.

The next point is important because it is a tool that will serve, support and strengthen your content, however without it, you could end up not establishing enough facts and materials to convince your client that you are indeed the one to provide a solution to their problems with the level of content you have provided. I am talking about **RESEARCH**. There are a certain amount of people that make the mistake of not doing effective research when writing their book or creating content. The problem with not doing research is that you will lack the right information which then leads to the book being unsuccessful and you being questioned as an expert in your field. There will no point writing a book that is going to be irrelevant in your industry leaving your potential client feeling unsatisfied after reading your book, and have no interest at all of working with you. Whatever content you are writing, conducting thorough research is an excellent idea. Researching a book can take many forms, but the best writers make sure if they are writing about something, they know about it.

Readers need to believe that what they are reading is the truth, even if at the beginning they did not believe, you need to provide enough information for them to buy into your beliefs around the topic. Having the ability to provide information that will enable your readers to get immersed into the world of content you have created is crucial to the readers' value of the content that you shared in your book, and thorough research is how you make it so. In order to do this effectively you also need to get a clear idea of some of the questions your readers would like answered. The research to be done in order to make this possible is not necessarily about going to the library, but from my experience, I have found the following ways can also be very effective to ask questions surrounding various topics you will be covering in your book.

- Survey Monkey
- Questionnaires
- Social media
- Feedback forms from current clients
- Search engines
- Forums
- Interviews

These are some of the ways that will enable you to uncover the pains, problems or unanswered questions individuals may have and address them in your book rather than producing a book that does not relate to your business, audience or undermines your authority in your field.

The third point to make a keen note of when completing your P.O ensures that you don't just provide important information for your reader, but also become an influencer to them so that they buy into you the author, and inevitably will then buy into your products and services. This is **IMPACT**. You need to ensure that your book not only makes an impact on your business but also on your clients. You want to be seen as an influencer and captivate your audience with your story and content. When writing your story make sure to pull your reader into it by using the power of description so that they can envision themselves being there with you. It is very important to include your own personal experiences; this is what will help to position you. I need you to make note of a very valid fact, you don't have to actually be an expert on a topic to write about it or have impact, but if you write with impact, you can then be seen as an expert. Secondly, you need to write with authenticity, so you need to ensure that what you are addressing is meaningful to you in some way. Another important way that you can ensure that your book makes an impact is to offer actionable tips that the reader can implement and action throughout the book. One crucial point some authors miss is the ability to interact with the reader to ensure that you keep their attention, and you can do this by asking rhetorical questions, sharing diagrams, giving them activities and exercises to do. With regards to the book making an impact to you and your business, I have stated a scenario below that would be good for you to read and answer the related questions.

Your readers:

- How can I captivate my readers?
- If I saw my book on a shelf would the cover interest me to pick it up?
- Do I have the content that will enable them to consider me as a 'go to person?'
- What support can I provide to help the reader to offer incredible value?

You and/or your business:

Let's say that your book has now been published and it is two years' on. I want you to make note of what has transpired since and how it has benefited you and your business.

- Did it help to establish and position you as an authority or expert in your field?

- Did it assist in creating a platform for you as well as bring opportunities for you as a speaker?

- Did potential clients find, connect and sign up for your products or services?

- Did it get you massive media attention?

- Was it able to help boost your brand?

- Did it increase your company's value and income?

So instead of writing aimlessly, you want to ensure that you are making an impact with the information you are delivering, that the content is carefully put together using a formula that will help you pass your information clearly, concisely but more importantly, beneficially.

The next step is the **T** in the **W.R.I.T.E** AUTHORS JOURNEY and if you don't have this, you may end up procrastinating and writing for the next several years without completion. However, with it you will be able to guide yourself in order to ensure that you actually put the work in to get your book done. I am talking about having a **TIMEFRAME**. What do I mean by this? It is to ensure that you set a deadline around the time that it will take to complete the book along with the necessary tasks involved. Why is this important? The problem with not setting a timeframe is that it can cause unproductive use of time to occur and that means unnecessary delays, and a book that was meant to take six months ends up taking two years or never actually happening at all. You need to set timeframes by creating goals and mini-goals which you will also set deadlines to follow. The reason for doing this is to breakdown each stage and the processes that you need to carry out. For example, have a look below.

COMPLETE BOOK – DURATION 6 MONTHS

TASK	PERIOD
Book Cover & write Introduction	MONTH 1
Title / Bio / Summary / Image	2 weeks
ISBN/Barcode/ Write Intro	2 weeks
Research	MONTH 2
Interviews (if required) Resources (Foreword / Editor / Internal Designer etc.)	4 weeks
(Timeframe daily tasks to complete towards achieving this result)	
Chapter 1 / 2 / 3 / 4 / 5	MONTH 3 (1 Chapter per week)
Chapter 5 / 6 / 7 / 8 /	MONTH 4 (1 Chapter per week)
Chapter 9 /10 or Final touches / Editor	MONTH 5
Layout Design / Publish / Proof copy	MONTH 6

Everyone works at a different time and pace; you don't have to set aside a whole day to be able to write although obviously that would help you to complete quickly. However, having that mindset might make you tell yourself that you do not have the time to commit. It is really about having consistency and doing a bit daily. It could be before you go to or get out of bed, on the bus, in the car (using a voice recorder), or setting aside time to write. Having a notebook with me at all times came in handy and at one point, I did not even realise the amount of content I had written until compiling it together to type, which did make it easier. Having a daily deadline to do your work and regular writing time will definitely help you finish writing your book. Scheduling time ahead will ensure you keep to the deadline; don't let yourself off the hook easily by skipping deadlines.

The final point in this chapter is important because without it you will continue waffling on with unnecessary information after you have shared the content that you needed the reader to have. However, by following it you will be able to complete the writing of the book and not get stuck on perfectionism. I am talking about having an **EXIT STRATEGY**. The problem with not having an exit strategy is that it may lead to the author never finishing the book, overwriting or allowing perfectionism to creep in. As you approach the end of your book writing project, keep in mind that it will be hard for you to bring it to a close as you will always be telling yourself that there is something else that you need to write or have not done. This is where outlining your content ahead comes in handy as this will ensure that you have listed all that you want to cover in the book and once all areas have been ticked then that is your cue to exit. No matter what, finish the book! Keep to your deadline. You then have to release it to the world. Send it to the editor, publisher or do whatever you need to do to get it in front of people, just don't leave the manuscript on the laptop or keep going over it with the aim to perfecting it, as this will not get you or your book anywhere; being constantly judgmental of your writing will affect your book moving forward.

The decision is yours to either start your journey on the wrong foot or commence on the **W.R.I.T.E** Authors Journey.

Watch a video of me sharing tips in a Facebook community

CHAPTER THREE

The Magic Pen

This next step is where all the magic takes place and I am not talking about you closing your eyes, saying a few spells and then the content appears (ha-ha). Instead I am talking about having the right tips and effective strategies which will enable you to get the content out of your head and on to your blank paper or screen. Without you having the solution that I am about to cover, you may possibly become stuck, unsure of where to start or experience what they call the 'writers block.' However, if you use this formula you will be able to save a lot of time, dive into the right content and know exactly where to start, where you are going and take the direction in what you're writing to get you there. In order for this to happen I believe that you have to first have a plan, you need to create a thorough plan of your book ensuring that it takes the right angle. You need to plan the chapters, topics, and information that you will be covering in each chapter. This should go as far as to cover the quotes, examples, diagrams or exercises that you want to use and share. Why? Well here's the thing, the more thorough your plan, the less time you will consume working on your book. In order to plan and have the magic flow throughout your book writing process and have ease in creating content I created a process called **The Non-F.I.C.T.I.O.N Content Constructor**.

> When you have a clear roadmap it makes the journey a lot easier

The first point will enable you to clearly map out all that will be required of you ahead; you will be able to see how it all flows and falls into place. Many people say or think that when writing a book, you just get up and start writing, but I believe that is definitely not the case. I believe that when you have a clear roadmap it makes the journey a lot easier. Let's think about it for a minute; you are going on a journey, you know exactly where it is that you want to get to, but you have no clear direction on how to get there. A few things will definitely happen. You will either get stuck, lost or end up giving up. You may find your way, but it will take a very long time. In the name of the formula you can see that an acronym was used in the word NON-F.I.C.T.I.O.N so let's take a look at what it stands for and how this solution can help you plan the content for your business book. The first step is that you need to have a framework. Regardless of what book you are writing, whether it is a business or passion book, a framework is needed.

FRAMEWORK

Books are segmented into three sections:

- Front Matter
- Body
- Back Matter

Below I have given an idea of what each section consists of. I believe that it is crucial to get your book structure completed once the mapping has been completed.

The Front Matter

This is the first few pages when you open a book. This is sometimes skipped by readers, but it does include some important information on behalf of the author and publisher. Let's have a look at what you need to include in the front matter.

- **Frontispiece**: (This is optional): a decorative illustration printed on the side facing the title page.
- **Title page**: The title and author's name as it appears on the cover and spine should be inserted here.
- **Copyright page**: It's found on the reverse of the title page and contains edition dates, copyrights, typefaces, ISBN, publisher and sometimes the printers name.
- **Dedication page**: (This is optional): This is where the author names the person or people for whom they have written the book.

- **Epigraph**: (This is optional): This is a phrase, quotation, or excerpt from a poem and can serve as a preface.

- **Table of contents**: A list of chapter headings, subheadings (which is optional), along with the respective page numbers, and the contents should include all sections that come after the table of contents.

- **Foreword**: (This is optional): This is an introduction written by an individual that you have chosen, preferably someone of status to help attract your potential readers.

- **Preface**: (This is optional): This is an introduction written by you, the author. It shows the primary objective, how the book came into being or provides context for its creation.

- **Acknowledgment**: (This is optional) This is an acknowledgment to those who contributed to the creation of the book or your journey.

The Body

The anatomy of a book is something called the **body**. For both you the author and the readers, this is where the magic happens.

Let's now look at what the body of a book consists of:

- **Introduction or Prologue**: In non-fiction books you will find introductions, whilst novels at times have prologues.

- **Chapters**: Chapters split your book into segments or, as a business book, can be the breakdown of your business modules. This is normally where most of the writing takes place and where you have to be mindful not to get carried away. However, remember that you want to deliver enough content to be seen as an expert but also leave them incomplete so that they will still want to learn more from you. You also want to ensure that you do not end up writing an encyclopaedia. Books can end in various ways; epilogue, afterword, postscript or conclusion. A non-fiction book is commonly ended using a conclusion which is a summary of the core ideas and concepts covered in the chapters

The Back Matter

The back matter (which is also called the end matter) is located at the back of the book and is used to give readers additional information about the book.

Below is what the back matter consists of:

- **Appendix or Addendum**: This is extra information based on the content you have covered in the body.

- **Chronology**: A list of the events in sequential order; this may be helpful for the reader. This is sometimes presented in the appendix.

- **Notes**: These are normally organized by chapter and should have been progressively created throughout the writing stage of the book.

- **Copyright permissions**: If you've sought permission to reproduce song lyrics, artwork, or extended extracts from other books, you may be required to attribute the credit in this section.

- **Glossary**: Definitions of words that are of importance to the work, and sorted in alphabetical order. The entries include places and characters, which is common for longer works of fiction.

- **Bibliography and Reference List**: A breakdown of sources cited in the work. These chronologically listed items should have already been attributed in the book.

- **Contributors**: A list of people you are acknowledging who aided you in researching or writing the book.

- **Index**: This is a list of terms used in the book and pages where they are used; non-fiction books normally have indices.

- **About the Author**: This is the right place to mention a bit about yourself, who you are, what you do and a final call to action to visit your website and social networks.

INFORMATION

You will find that a content framework will save you time planning and writing your book. The time you spend planning and creating the framework for your book will be a benefit with regards to the time you save writing it. I believe that having a strong content plan will also help you create a better selling content, enabling you to position yourself and later on create other products or services. This is indeed powerful as it will make the content of your book obvious to prospective readers the moment, they commence reading. Your book content framework will also make it easier for you to promote your book or business.

Additionally, converting it into articles, blog posts, presentations, and talks will in turn drive more clients to your business and not just any clients, but your ideal clients. Now let's take a look at the quality of information that you will provide. Many pay attention to the quantity, the amount of words or pages, but not enough on the information. If your book is a 'how to' book, or a book that is going to help the reader solve a problem, then think about the process you use or offer to help your readers achieve the results they want. You firstly need to ensure that you share your expert positioning story especially as in today's society, positioning is everything. Expert positioning is one of the fastest ways to increase business and become the authority in your field. You then want to cover the pains, solutions and steps that the readers need to take in order to achieve their desired results. There are a few things to keep at the forefront and those are:

- What is their pain?
- What are their needs?
- What is their pleasure?
- What steps or process would you take them through?
- What have you already done for others?

Let us now see how you can then group those ideas on your map into the steps of your process in order to create a framework for your book.

Firstly, share your expert positioning story, this is what will connect you to your readers and position you as an expert which is critical to your book.

Your story not only connects you to your audience but will also establish authority, inspire hope, and will motivate the reader.

- Share your challenge or pain that started you on the journey.
- Enable the reader to relate to you.
- Your catalyst moment.
- The transformation that you made.
- Your experience and source of knowledge to demonstrate why you are the expert?
- Share your story of success or your client's success with you via case study.
- Share your trial, errors and vulnerability (so that the reader recognises that you are human.)
- State the pains that your clients go through that your business solves, (this could be modules that you cover in your business which will formulate your chapters.)

CHAPTERS AND CONTENT

{ EXPERT STORY}	{PAIN POINT 2}	{PAIN POINT 3}	{PAIN POINT 4}	{PAIN POINT 5}

{ PAIN POINT 6}	{PAIN POINT 7}	{PAIN POINT 8}	{PAIN POINT 9}	{PAIN POINT 10}

This is where you will now break down and list what skills or solutions your readers would need to solve each pain point. I have given a simple mapping example below.

a. List all the pain points of your clients.

b. List the skills or solutions for each pain below that point.

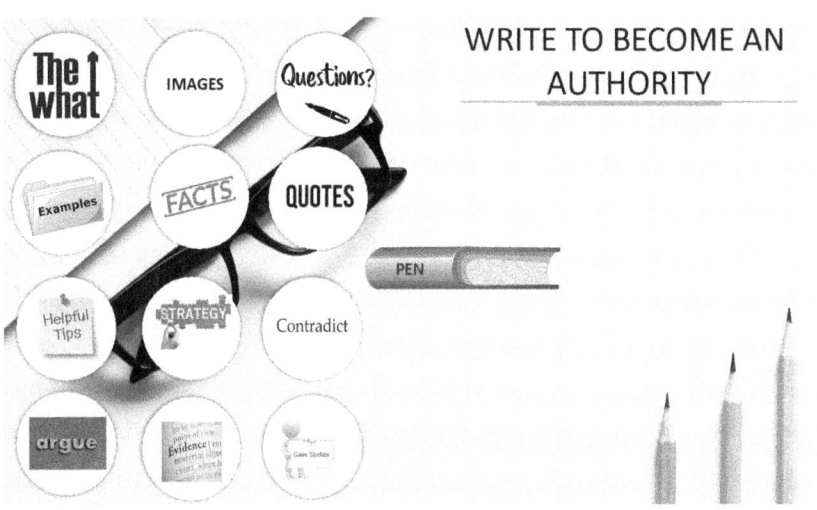

Now that your book structure is set you need to start creating the magic. You will commence by writing content on each pain point and solution using the following:

Creating content is indeed where the true work comes in and the best way to extract content is by asking questions regarding the point you are addressing. For instance:

What is it?

Why is it important?

What will happen when they have it (benefits) and will happen without it (disadvantages)?

Then you also want to educate the reader. Now what do I mean by this? When I say educate, I mean that you will now pass valuable content as well as your beliefs concerning the topic to the reader. This is essential, especially if your book is a 'how to book' or 'self-help book.' The reader wants to learn what will bridge the gap to get them from where they are now to where they desire to be. This is where you now ask and answer questions that the reader would ask if they were standing in front of you by sharing statistics, facts, examples and/or diagrams/images etc. You would additionally include universal experiences, stories, examples and also get them to do activities such as questionnaires and exercises etc. Allow the reader to be able to relate to your point just the same as you would do if you were having a 'one to one' conversation with them. You also need to give the reader something to take away, whether it be tips, strategies, quotes or something that will make a difference or that they can go and implement straight away. Throughout your book, I also highly recommend that you embed CTA's (call to actions), getting the reader to click on your website, subscribe to your social media pages or channel. You may wish to offer little freebies, reports or PDFs which they can access via one of these platforms, this will help drive traffic to your pages. A very classy way of doing this is to create QR codes for the reader to scan which will take them straight to the URL where they can then download templates or complete questionnaires.

You need to make your content appealing, therefore creating a bit of controversy around what people normally say about the point you are writing on that you don't agree with. You want to rant about it, state the truths and give evidence by showing examples of case studies, preferably of you, a client or a well-known individual. Ask yourself a lot of questions. Ask clients and other people questions. You can do this by using Survey Monkey, social media, creating polls and also using Quora to find out what the buzz is around your topic or the many questions you can answer in your book; this will also make sure that your content is relevant to your target audience. At all times think about the process of helping your readers achieve the results they want.

Once you've broken down every point in your plan and gone into as much detail as possible, you'll see that because you've planned so thoroughly, there isn't a whole much left to write. Essentially, you're just filling the space in between your notes. Describe your points at a high level and do the same for each example. Include links and references that you can use to look up more information if you desire to go into more depth.

Another way of getting content is by writing an anthology book which, as stated in Wikipedia, 'is a book or other collection of selected writings by various authors, usually in the same literary form, of the same period, or on the same subject' or you can have what we call 'contributors.' In this book you will come across contributors who have shared their knowledge and expertise around the topic I am writing on which has added value to the content. You do not have to know everything as there are others who have the knowledge, information and different experiences around the very topic you are writing on, so you don't have to re-invent the wheel but instead collaborate. This will indeed save time and possibly money. One way of raising funds for the creation of your book is to sell a chapter to a contributor which will be a win-win situation; you provide the opportunity; the contributor provides the content. The contributor may want some visibility but is not ready or able to write their book or have enough funds to do so and therefore writing a chapter and paying a small fee may appeal to them. They will be in your book for the lifetime of the book, so it becomes a no-brainer.

Your next question may be 'how many words the book should consist of?' Remember, you are not writing an encyclopaedia, I cannot stress this enough. You are writing a marketing tool, a business card so it needs to appeal to even those who are not typical book readers. In my opinion, the standard non-fiction book should consist of no more than approximately 50,000 words.

A few final tips I would like to share when writing your content:

- When writing remove, yourself from distraction.
- Do not edit while you go along, that's the editor's job.
- Give yourself deadlines and stick to them.
- Do not be a perfectionist.
- Stay organised.
- Do not over think or believe you need to provide more information than is absolutely necessary.

- Do your research.

- Provide content that sells.

- Keep a list of helpful questions to ask yourself as you go along to assist with providing consistency in your writing.

- Do not compare yourself to others - get inspiration but not a reason to stop.

TITLES

Both your book title and names for your chapters should be clearly defined and support your content but also needs to draw attention or attract the interest of your reader. Based on the fact that this book is a business book, the name of your chapters should be congruent with the cause, and so this is where you will now go back to your mapping notes to see the pains addressed and name the chapters based on this. The reason for this is that as a business book the plan should be to create products or services on the back end therefore, you want your chapters to take on the shape of a module. For instance, every chapter in my book (including my story) has the ability to be used later whether to write a blog or share as a free PDF etc.

Choose a single word or a few words that sums up the book or chapters, preferably around the pain or solution you are writing on.

Make the title draw attention. Be mindful to ensure that it describes that what is 'on the tin' is actually 'in the tin', but also have fun and make it witty, for example, 'The Magic Pen'.

You can have a play on words but do not let it be too vague i.e. AUTHORITY'. Let the purpose of the book and chapters be evident in the title.

When writing the main title of your business book, having a subtitle is recommended as this is where the reader will have a clear understanding of what your book is about. Please pay attention. I said the words 'clear understanding.' If you are writing about property development, then your subtitle cannot be mentioning cars. You DO NOT want to confuse your potential readers. You should be going along the lines of a 'How to...' or '7 Tips to Subtitle,' demonstrating what it is that you will be showing them to do, where you are taking them from and eventually, where you are taking them to, which is the main issue that you are addressing for your clients and where it is that you are helping them to be.

Examples below are titles from my books:

- 'Overcome and Rise Above – How to Turn the Downside of Your Challenges to the Upside of Renewing Your Life.'
- 'Rise Above and Believe – It's Do or Lie – How to Get Rid of Excuses and Create the Life You Desire.'
- 'Authority – How to Write Your Business Book and Use it as a Marketing Tool.'

IMAGES

When it comes to images, many authors underestimate the importance that pictures, and illustrations contribute in adding something extra to their story. A picture can often say a lot more than a thousand words. It sometimes creates more impact than the paragraph you have written. You need to take into account the fact that you want to appeal to your target market. Visual individuals depend on their sight and imagination to make sense of the world. Using pictures also breaks the book up and gives it life. With regards to using images in your content without permission, I would suggest that you create your own by using a photographer or illustrator. You need to ensure that a good resolution is used so that it is of good quality after printing. The recommendation is to ensure that images are at least at a resolution of 300 dpi. This however you may find to be the expensive route and so for a more economical option, a royalty-free stock photo will need to be used.

BOOKCOVER

The above also relates to the images that you are using for your front cover, even more so, as this is the first thing that the reader sees.

Here are some websites from which to download stock photos:

- iStock
- Shutterstock
- Free Images
- Getty Images
- Stockvault
- Photogen

However, make sure to read the terms on the website before using the pictures. If you download a photo from the internet and use it in your book or cover, you need to check if it is copyright protected.

OWNERSHIP

When writing your content, a common question that comes to mind concerns copyright, plagiarism or the ownership of your material. As stated by Wikipedia, here are some definitions below:

Copyright is the use of works protected by copyright law without permission, infringing certain exclusive rights granted to the copyright holder, such as the right to reproduce, distribute, display or perform the protected work, or to make derivative works. The copyright holder is typically the work's creator, or a publisher or other business to whom copyright has been assigned. Copyright holders routinely invoke legal and technological measures to prevent and penalize copyright infringement.

Plagiarism is the "wrongful appropriation" and "stealing and publication" of another author's "language, thoughts, ideas, or expressions" and the representation of them as one's own original work.

Fair use, in its most general sense, a fair use is any copying of copyrighted material done for a limited and "transformative" purpose, such as to comment upon, criticize, or parody a copyrighted work. Such uses can be done without permission from the copyright owner.

Two regular questions I have come across are:

What can I actually use?

When is permission needed?

To answer this, there are no set rules with regards to how much you can really use from existing works. However, to be on the safe side you should exercise caution and keep it short to approximately three hundred words. In regard to writing about real people when sharing examples or case studies to clarify or emphasise your facts or opinions, you can use the names of real people as long as the material is not damaging to their reputation. In order to use quotes in a book, provided that you credit the person who created it or spoke it then no permission is required. For example:

"The Pessimist Sees Difficulty in Every Opportunity. The Optimist Sees Opportunity in Every Difficulty."
– Winston Churchill.

These are the main things to consider when writing your book, unless you want to take things a step further and actually legally make your book an intellectual property. This is a route not many authors bother to take but if what you have created and the system with which you have shared the book is your own unique solution, then it may be worth doing.

NATURE

What do I mean by nature and why is it important? The word nature in the Oxford Dictionary means '*The innate or essential qualities or character of a person, thing or animal or characteristics as an influence on or determinant of personality.*'

So, what do I mean by nature when writing a book? It's knowing the character and impact you want the book to have on the reader, and the emotions that you want coming through. This is important because it will help the reader to relate, engage and take the action that you desire of them. The best way to allow your book to show its true nature is by the power of emotion. This is highly influential, it is good to make the reader at times laugh, smile and even cry. You want your book to make an impact and this is empowered by the use of emotions. I, for instance, love sharing quotes because I have realised that it helps me to reflect, pause and pay close attention; this may also be the same for some of you. I also like humour because it tends to break up the information, giving the reader time to breathe. Here is the thing, people in general love to be touched and moved by what they hear or read, especially something that challenges or gives an opportunity to make a change in their lives. As much as you want to pass content, you also need to do it in a way that empowers and stimulates the reader to take action. Therefore, it is very important to know what character you want your book to impart. Impactful? Humorous? Enlightening? Motivational? Or a combination of all. If you want to reach your reader's emotions, you need to write emotion-evoking content and so allow your book to take on that persona. Yes, it is a book but don't underestimate what it has the ability to do. Some words are triggers in themselves and can be used to set off the reader and stir up emotions that bring on a complete transformation.

Let's say you are sharing stories in your book whether it be as examples, real or even anecdotal stories. You should use a setting to influence the reader and deepen their emotional response or state. Give a clear description of the scene, the smell, audio, visual and emotions. Coax the reader into the scene by allowing them to create an image in their mind and therefore place themselves there.

Tips:

- Don't let your book be all content. Include stories and anecdotes - this will actually help the reader believe that they can also achieve similar results as others have.

- Use emotions – this will help the reader to relate and take action.

- Share images. Paint pictures in the readers' minds - this will help to hold their attention and keep it interesting.

- Keep your avatar or target market in mind – this will help you to write using the persona and words they need in order to bring effect.

- Create the mood for your book – this will make impact.

This brings us to the end of this chapter, and I do hope that you will use the information provided to write amazing content for your book, but more importantly, make an impact and be seen as the expert.

Do's

- Carry a journal with you at all times.
- Get feedback from your community, clients and raving fans.
- Ensure that your content relates to your clients.
- Set goals and deadlines.

Keep your avatar or target market in mind

DON'Ts

- Pay attention to how much other people are writing.
- Allow yourself to get distracted by other activities when writing.
- Try to get it absolutely perfect.
- Forget to map out your content.

CHAPTER FOUR

Publishing Success

---

*"The world's greatest achievers have been those
who have always stayed focussed on their goals
and have been consistent in their efforts."*
~ Dr. Roopleen

You have now completed the exciting part of creating your content; let's now address the steps needed regarding publishing. The last thing you want to do is write your manuscript and then begin to procrastinate by continuously revisiting the script. It is now time to publish. As an author, knowing **how to publish your manuscript** is very important and you have the control when selecting publishers or the publishing process you desire to take. Finding and selecting the right publishing process can at times become frustrating, and if the right choices are not made, it can have an adverse effect later on down the line.

In order to assist my clients with this I have created a formula called 'The Professional Publishing Process.' This will help you to not only make the right choices in order get your book published but also the most economical and professional way. In this formula we look at the 3 D's.

The first D enables you to make the right choice for yourself and your book. However, without it you may end up not only becoming frustrated but may also lose money in the process. I am talking about Decision. Making the right decision is crucial when it comes to the next steps of the process. The first decision to make is how do you want to publish? The traditional way of publishing or self-publishing with an intermediary? Whatever decision you make there is no right or wrong answer as there have been successful authors using either options. The task at hand is for me to now explain the various ways and then for you to make the ultimate decision as to which option is most beneficial for you.

WHAT IS TRADITIONAL PUBLISHING?

This is an established system in which to get a book deal and involves submission to agents over a period of time which normally comes with quite a few rejections and then maybe hopefully acceptance. The agent submits your manuscript to publishers. After numerous rejections you will then get to sign a contract which will be followed by more of your time editing, going over figures and the contract before continuing. The publisher organizes editing, proofreading, design, marketing and distribution with no upfront costs to you, the author. This process can come about in two ways. You may be approached to write a book for them which would be great but does come with the status of already being known, or you can approach the publishers and offer them your manuscript. An advance would be given but this does depend on the book and your situation. If they commissioned the book, you might only get a one-off payment, or they'll pay you a small percentage of the sales once the book is out. There are always pros and cons with any decision you make and I will share some of the main ones regarding traditional publishing below.

Pros

- No upfront financial costs.
- Exposure and support.
- Easier to get your book onto retailers' shelves.
- More validation.

Cons

- Extremely slow process that can take years to complete.
- Deal can end up being cancelled.
- Lack of control over your book.
- Low royalty rates.

WHAT IS SELF-PUBLISHING?

Self-publishing is the publication of your manuscript without the involvement of an established publisher. So perhaps you are wondering 'is self-publishing for me?' There are several things to consider in order to make that decision. With self-publishing, you are the one that organises the editing, proofreading, design and the completion of all of the steps needed in order to get your book out to the world including the marketing and arranging the distribution. This can be costly or actually very cost effective if you know what you are doing and take the right action. Many authors turn to self-publishing because they want a cheaper process and more control over their book. However, the challenge with self-publishing without guidance is that the quality of the end product may not be to the standard that will truly represent your business. Remember, never lose sight of the fact that the book will be representing you and therefore needs to be of a certain quality. The majority of the time authors, when self-publishing, get thrown into the world of templates and may not have or know the correct strategy on how to get the right editors and designers to finalise the finished product. The next challenge is ensuring that your book gets the right publicity, and all of this is what will determine the success that your book will have in the end. At times the choice of self-publishing can cause you to start off with a relatively cheap budget that may end up spiralling out of control and cost you more in the long run. One of the most utilised platforms adopted by authors for self-publishing is Amazon. This works for those individuals who are happy to use templates etc, and who are not too fussed about getting that 'personalised' touch to their books. Self-publishing, when done correctly, is especially good for first-time authors as not only do you get to remain in control and be your own boss, but you can get your work out there without worrying about budgets, time delays or the endless red tape and ownership.

Pros

- You are the boss and make all the decisions.
- Can be more cost effective.
- Higher royalties.
- Own copyright.
- Guaranteed acceptance.

Cons

- Unnecessary loss of money.
- Low quality with end product.
- Delays and possibility of getting stuck in a rut.
- Lack the correct information.
- Lack exposure and marketing.
- No agent or representation.

WHAT IS A SELF-PUBLISHING INTERMEDIARY?

A self-publishing intermediary is a service provided by a publisher asking for payment upfront unlike traditional publishers. It's a combination of self-publishing and having a mentor or company to help you on the journey. This is the category that my publishing academy falls into. I offer this process on two levels; one, by coaching the author through the self-publishing journey by helping them with the 'how to steps' of sourcing editors, designers and the strategies for promoting your book. The next level is providing a more handheld experience in which I work with you on creating the content and provide all of the other services such as the editing, proofreading, design and promotion, in other words, the complete package in order to get your book out there and within your hands. Companies such as mine can come in many different shapes and forms. Some of them are reputable companies and unfortunately, some are not. You may be asking what then makes my service unique. The first thing is that the programme was created by me and so is one of its kind, secondly, I do not work with templates; each programme is bespoke and so would be based on your specific needs and not generic. When it comes to writing a book, I do not believe that one size should fit all, especially when it is a business book which has different target markets, branding and also where the author has a different lifestyle. This leads me to another service that appeals to some, largely due to the fact that time is not one that they have plenty of. If you fall into this category I then work with you to create the content but with your own spin, feel and knowledge within it which is obtained through interviews; the content is then created on this basis. Another very crucial unique selling point is the fact that I utilise my skills as a performance coach in order to hold you accountable and also take you through the process of extracting content from you that you possibly did not even recognise or were aware that you had; this is normally handy in ensuring that your book gets done effectively and within the timescale you desire it to be published by. This option to publish your book is normally great for most people and is a viable option for most authors in today's society. I would, however, advise that you read any contract thoroughly to ensure that despite what they may say to you verbally, you actually own the copyright to your book and that the editing and design offered is well worth your money and not just a templated procedure. I would advise you that under no circumstances sign away your copyright to anyone who asks you to pay.

Pros

- You are the boss and make all the decisions.
- Budget friendly.
- Higher royalties.
- Ownership of copyright.
- Guaranteed acceptance.
- Handheld support on the journey.
- Versatile publishing packages
- No time constraints.
- Experts to handle all the technicalities.
- Assistance with the creation of the content.

Cons

- Unnecessary loss of money.
- Low quality of end product.
- Misinformation.
- Less marketing support.
- Upfront fee.
- No agent or representation.

As you can see from the above, there are a lot of things to keep in mind and why the decision making process is crucial when taking into account all the pros, cons and what works best for you.

The next **D** to explore, especially if you are self-publishing, is very important because if you don't, you may end up limiting your book's potential. However, if you get this right, (which is also based on making the right decision), you will be able to generate sales and get your book into more hands. This is **Distribution**, which is the process of getting your book out there and into the hands of your customers. There are 4 types of distribution:

Print-on-demand is the newest form of distributing and widely used. Print-on-demand books are printed directly from electronic files such as PDFs and enables the ability to print single copies of a book when purchased by a customer. This is the procedure sites such as Amazon use. The client purchases the book and their copy is then printed on request and shipped to the customer. This kind of distribution is very economical as it saves space, printing in bulk and has the advantage of only producing exact quantities therefore eliminating the necessity of a large investment and inventory.

Trade distribution A trade distributor is a partner company which takes over the tasks and responsibilities of selling your books to trade accounts such as bookstores and wholesalers like Waterstones and W.H. Smith. This is due to their size and so is often a better leveraging power to sell books, get good placement for the books they represent and also the payment process. Trade distribution normally comes at a higher cost and so it is generally recommended that a minimum of 1500-3000 copies should be printed in order to reduce the unit price.

Wholesale distribution refers to the use of established book wholesalers such as IngramSpark and Baker and Taylor, in order to provide fulfilment of book orders from bookstores and libraries. The ability to have your book available through a wholesaler is normally an exciting one for authors. Wholesale distribution setup is generally a preliminary to bookstore marketing. Therefore, if you are in the UK and looking to get your book into stores such as Waterstones or W.H. Smith, then signing up with distributors such as IngramSpark would be recommended.

Consignment distribution is normally sometimes recommended for self-publishers to sell copies of their book on a consignment basis to their local and special interest bookstores. The terms of consignment differ from store to store, but in general consignment means that the store will stock copies for a designated period of time.

MY RECOMMENDATION

Based on my experience, print-on-demand book distribution is the most straightforward by making use of the technology to print your books rather than investing in a print run where you produce hundreds or even thousands of books at a time. I did this for my first book and ended up having an attic full of books and not knowing what to do with them. Luckily for me, I was able to really make a push and truly went radical with getting my book out there and it achieved a bestseller status. However, this is not an economical or wise move and causes unnecessary upfront spend.

Print-on-demand printing means that your book isn't printed until someone orders and pays for it. As I mentioned above, take this into consideration. If your book is only printed when it is ordered, that then reduces your risk, the disadvantage however is that you are probably not going to see your books sitting on bricks-and-mortar retail shelves. Obviously, you do still have to order a quantity in bulk for your keeping and also if you are planning to do a book launch or speak at events where you can sell them.

If you are considering the print-on-demand route, then you have two key distributors to consider:

IngramSpark

Amazon KDP

You can use both distributors in order to maximise your reach, but you would have to purchase an additional ISBN as you cannot use an Amazon provided ISBN or the same ISBN on Amazon with any that you want to distribute using IngramSpark. If you really have a desire to get your book into book stores then you should definitely use IngramSpark. Set your discount rate at 55% and make the books returnable as this is the industry standard arrangement if you want bookstores to purchase. If you follow these steps distribution will definitely be an area where you will have no concerns.

The final **D** in the equation is very significant in your book publishing process because this is where the numbers now come into play. I am talking about **D**ividends. This is where you have to now pay attention to the money you will make from the sales of your book. However, be reminded that a huge amount of money is not really from selling individual copies of your book but more from what you can create on the back-end of the book; this does not mean that you will not pay attention to the income that can be earned from your book sales.

Firstly, let's look at another common question that I get asked. 'How do I set the right retail price?' Well this involves many factors, but how you price your book is ultimately your decision. You just need to set an ideal price so that you can sell your books competitively and still make a bit of profit. This is where some more research comes in so that you can compare similar books and compare prices as you do not want to set your price too high as opposed to other books in a comparative genre. You also don't want to price your book so low that the printing costs eat up all of your royalties.

There are 4 C's that you can do:
- Check local book stores.
- Case online retailers.
- Consider your target market.
- Compare other books within your category.

A book that contains a fair amount of research, statistics, endnotes, charts, graphs, a colour interior or other details makes it valuable and unique and therefore it is reasonable for you to price the book higher than average. However, if you are looking to make money from the back-end of the book then you need to be more focused on getting the book into your client's hands instead of pricing it too high so that they don't buy it. You may also look at running a campaign where you will offer the book for free but charge enough for postage and packing in order to cover the printing costs. In the UK, authors who have written a business book tend to price their books between the range of £9.99 - £14.99.

Three main ways that dividends normally come from book sales are:

- The Advance.

  What is typically referred to as a 'book advance' is actually an advance against future royalties. This is normally offered by traditional publishers who will give the author an advance against royalties based on what they think the book will earn. A publisher calculates this based on:

- The size of the publisher.

- Historical performance of similar books.

- The author's track record.

- The content and the topic that the book covers.

- Royalties from book sales.

- Royalties.
These are basically the author's cut of their book sales and usually works out to be a percentage of the retail price. If you are with a traditional publisher your contract will specify royalty rates for hardcover, trade paper, large print and electronic editions etc. It will also specify the terms under which they'll pay your royalties. If you use Amazon KDP, royalties are paid every month, approximately 60 days after the end of the month in which they were earned.

- Reselling the Book Yourself.
You are able to buy your book for at least half of your retail price and sell it anywhere such as on your website or at events etc. However, with traditional publishers there are certain restrictions applied on how and where you can sell books yourself. This does at times come in handy and can drum up a few quid.

Beyond all of this the key point to remember about publishing is that it takes a lot of hard work and thought process. Some will have you believe that publishing a book is easy because they just write, publish and print, but that is not all it takes. The question is, do you want to just publish your book or have true publishing success? Whether you believe it or not there is a massive difference and if you doubt it then have a look at all those that say that they have authored a book. You will note that for one, they are a successful author and the other, just an author – I guess it's for you to decide which category you want to be in. The work after publishing doesn't stop for you. Granted, it is a lot of work to create, format and set up the book, but once that's done, it's time to get your skates on and step it up a notch.

CHAPTER FIVE

The Perfect P.R.I.N.T

There are a lot of things involved in book printing and much to consider. However, the printing process you choose has a significant influence on the final quality of your book. In this chapter we are going to take a look at some areas of the book creation process that many authors do not pay close enough attention to despite the fact that if you get this aspect wrong, it can cause a dilemma in the final stage of your book.

PROOFREAD

Why is proofreading important? What tends to happen after being on the journey of writing your book is that now you are coming closer to the end, excitement tends to creep in which can then lead to shortcuts in order to get the book completed and in your hand. Unknown to many, there is a marked difference between getting your book edited and proofread as they are often mistaken for each other. Proofreading is the process that takes place at the proof stage of your book whereas the editing is done at the manuscript stage, and involves correcting grammatical errors, mistakes, inconsistencies and verifying facts etc. Proofreading is more about making sure that all editorial changes are completed. The best way to perform the proofreading process is to wait until the proof pages of your finished book are returned to you. You should read through your manuscript with minute detail and mark any corrections that you may see. Some people use red markers to make it more distinct or you can hire a professional proofreader to carry out the task for you; an option that I strongly believe you should explore. Even if your manuscript was professionally edited, I would still advise you to get it carefully proofread and checked. If you or the editor go through the manuscript, there is still the chance of there being errors as the manuscript can become so familiar that minor errors and typos can easily be overlooked and therefore having fresh eyes to take another look can be very beneficial. This may take more time than you want, and I have seen authors, that due to the time constraints, refuse to carry out this process and then end up being frustrated when they get their book and notice the hidden errors, so the extra time in the end is worth it.

A few tips when proofreading:

Look from the outside in. The person reading your book may not know you so when proofreading, put yourself in the readers' shoes so that instead of reading it as the author, read it as a stranger to ensure that your message comes across clearly and accurately.

Patterns – Keep an eye out for patterns or common mistakes in your writing.

Spell check – Do not rely on computer software to make the corrections for you as it won't catch every mistake.

Take your time – You may end up overlooking mistakes if you rush it. There may be some obvious errors staring right back at you that you may not notice, so focus.

Grammar and punctuation – Using words in the wrong context and punctuation marks in the incorrect place could send a bad message to your reader, especially the perfectionists. Some will be more interested in your message whilst others will be more inclined to pay attention to every little error in detail.

You need to check every fine detail but at the same time DO NOT be a perfectionist!

Blank pages - In a non-fiction book, you should leave blank pages where necessary so that chapters will start on recto pages.

Spacing – Ensure that your line spacing is consistent in every paragraph throughout the book and that with your word spacing, none of the lines are tighter or looser than others.

Fonts – You need to ensure that the font is consistent throughout the book.

Page numbers - Check that the page numbers in the table of contents are accurate and that the pages are numbered correctly.

Detail – You need to check every fine detail but at the same time DO NOT be a perfectionist!

REVISION

You have dealt with a lot to get to this point with some issues being very complicated and others being easy. You are drawing close to the end and now that you have completed the proofreading process it's time to do a final revision. This now involves you going through your book with a much softer glance. At this point you want to really look at your book, not the text, but instead, concentrate on everything else. Here are some of the things you should typically look for. You want to start to revision from the front and back covers of your book as they are very important to the book marketing process.

Some elements to revision:

Are you satisfied with the overall colours and design?

Is the title clearly visible and does it say what it is 'in the tin?'

Ensure that all content falls within the trimmed edges of the book. It is recommended to have 0.5″ minimum around the edges.

Ensure that the ISBN on the back cover matches the ISBN on your copyright page.

If you have included a category and price, are they correct?

Is your preference perfect bound or saddle stitched?

The interior page colour – white or cream coloured?

What finish do you want the cover to have - a gloss, matte or cloth cover? Each will have separate requirements and different pricing.

Duplex or single cover?

Hardback or paperback?

ISBN

What is an ISBN?

ISBN stands for International Standard Book Number and is a 13-digit number that identifies published books. There are five parts to an ISBN number. The current prefixes are 978 or 979. An ISBN identifies the registrant, title, edition and format of products used by publishers, bookstores and libraries etc and are important for ordering, sales reporting and inventory control and increases the chances of your book being found. The majority of bookstores will refuse to sell or feature your book if it's not listed within a warehouse database and your book needs to have an ISBN in order for this to be possible. Although some countries legally require the use of an ISBN to identify publications, it is not a form of legal or copyright protection. If you are publishing through Amazon, they will assign your book with an ISBN. On some occasions you might not even have to buy your ISBN number as some of the services offered to self-published authors by some of the print-on-demand publishing companies such as

IngramSpark and Smashwords include this is their pricing. If you are publishing a Kindle, then an ISBN is not required. However, if you want to purchase your unique ISBN then the place to go is Nielsen Book UK who provide a range of services to the book industry internationally, aiding the discovery and purchase, distribution and sales. They run the ISBN and SAN agencies for the UK and Ireland as well as providing search and discovery services for booksellers and libraries. I have been asked before if ISBN numbers expire and the answer to that is no, they do not, but they cannot be re-used once assigned to a book.

NUMBERS

There are a few important areas where numbers play an important role.

1. **Page Count**- Before you go to print you need to pay attention to and determine your page count as this contributes to pricing as well as cover size.

2. **Font Size** - When it comes to the interior of your book the design is very important as it needs to be presentable. There are certain elements where keen attention needs to be in order for your interior to achieve the look that you desire. Some common mistakes made tend to be on the interior of the book concerning both content and design. These include incorrect margin size, widow and orphan lines of text, wrong size and font type. Whatever you select for each element of your interior text design should remain consistent throughout the book. Whichever point typeface

you choose needs to be consistent with the exception of chapter title pages and sub-headings etc. The typical font size used by authors is 11 to 12 point font size unless you are producing 'large print' books, which are normally for readers with vision problems.

3. **Print Cost** - You always want to take into account how much it costs to print your book as this dictates how much you set as your retail price. If you are doing print-on-demand, your printing cost will be deducted from your retail price, so therefore your book royalties come from the retail price minus the cost of printing. Therefore, as I mentioned previously, you do not want to price your book so low that the printing costs eat up your royalties. Ensure that you make enough with each book to earn what you are paying for printing, postage and packaging and a little extra profit. There are a few factors that have to be considered in regard to printing costs. In this chapter, the majority of what I have covered will have a massive contribution to your printing cost.

4. **Book Size** – You have to know what size you want your book to be as this is also one of the elements that has an impact on the printing cost. Therefore, you need to decide this before you send your book off to print. I will be talking more about this below.

TRIM SIZE

The term used when talking about the dimensions of your printed book is called trim size. The most common sizes for a standard paperback are 5.5×8.5, 5×8, 6×9 and 4.25×7 inches. Books can come in all shapes and sizes, and it is normally down to the author and/or publisher to make the final decision on what size the book should be. The trim size determines the presentation of your book and influences both the interior and exterior of your book. The smaller your trim size, the more pages will be required for your content. It also impacts your book's spine - the more pages in your book, the thicker the spine will be.

The standard book sizes in publishing (in inches):
- **Fiction**: 4.25" x 6.87", 5" x 8", 5.25" x 8", 5.5" x 8.5", 6" x 9"
- **Novella**: 5" x 8"
- **Children's**: 7.5" x 7.5", 7" x 10", 10" x 8"
- **Textbooks**: 6" x 9", 7" x 10", 8.5" x 11"
- **Non-fiction**: 5.5" x 8.5", 6" x 9", 7" x 10"
- **Memoir**: 5.25" x 8", 5.5" x 8.5"

There's no clear-cut way to decide the trim size for your book, as it ultimately depends on your personal preference.

How do I choose my trim size?
- Base it on your word count.
- Tailor it to genre standards.
- Consider the impact on costs.

I believe that it is a good idea to produce books that you like the size of. Visually comparing other books in the same genre should assist in giving you a better sense of trim size for your own book. This may all sound complicated, but once you get it right you will have a book in your hand that you are not only satisfied with but confident about.

The printing process is intricate and there are some important steps to take into consideration before your content hits paper. Everything mentioned in this chapter is of great importance to the completion of your book and publication, so I therefore advise you to pay close attention to all the information that has been provided and take the time to research what works best for your book. Keep in mind not only the writing process but also what follows.

CHAPTER SIX

Promoting Strategies

Great, so that's some of the hard work done. Apologies if you thought that from now on it was all plain sailing as it isn't, there is yet more hard work to come.

The process of promoting your book and attaining visibility is equal to the challenging task of completing the actual writing of the book. I believe that this process is a crucial step in your book writing journey. Many authors produce a great book with awesome content that has the potential to change lives, but don't have a planned promotional strategy, and rather than being in the hands of potential readers, their book ends up collecting dust in a house, either under their bed, in the loft or stored in a shed. This is unlikely to gain them any clients or make any positive impact on their business. The majority of people tend to think that the promotion of a book doesn't start until it's completed. I will always rubbish that notion and say that it is utterly untrue. The promotion starts from the moment you have written your first word. It can be as simple as posting a social media comment such as, 'today I have started to work on my upcoming book.' This will start to create an immediate buzz about your book and will also hold you accountable, therefore, we will be exploring the very steps that you can take as an author to not only promote the book, but more importantly, to also raise your profile. Why is this important? Well the mistake that many authors make is that they split their attention between the book and book sales when they should actually both come hand in hand. You elevate the book and the book elevates you – that is the most effective way. You may be wondering how have I come to this conclusion? There is a well-known saying that states that 'the product speaks for itself.' But in a TV or radio interview, can a book speak for itself? No, it cannot, so therefore you need to be the voice of the book. Lifting your profile will subsequently help to lift your book. This is a crucial first point that I am going to address in this chapter as with this knowledge, you will be able to truly give leverage to your book and so boosting your value and your business. Without it, you will be amongst the many that are 'shed' or 'loft' authors with a book in hand but no income or visibility. That crucial first point is **PUBLICITY**.

PUBLICITY

This is all about you as an author getting noticed and known utilising various avenues within your market. Here is what IngramSpark, one of the biggest book distributors says about book publicity.

"**Book publicity** can be defined in one sentence: it is using the media as a conduit to spread word of an author and **book** to general and/or target audiences. ... You, the author, offer great material or ideas for a story, article, broadcast interview, podcast, etc., and the host or editor "plugs" your **book**.

With so many budding authors it has become more difficult for those authors to get noticed or have the ability to gain the publicity at the level that they would like and therefore find it an uphill struggle. The following tips are very handy in making sure that you do get that publicity. These steps helped me to get from being an unknown bookshelf author to where I am now having done multiple TV and radio interviews, podcasts and magazine articles.

1. Press release - (also otherwise known as media release). A press release is an announcement issued to the news media, (as well as other targeted publications), for the purpose of letting them know about your book. It is a way for you to get coverage for your book in publications or on TV and radio stations.

2. Personalise - This means that you need to recognise that your book cannot do all the work and so you have to make the effort to shine and shout about the book. As I mentioned before, as much as the book is helping you to build your brand, you also have to become your brand. Think about what it is that you will say in an interview. You will need to get the concept, understand the media demands, have the ability to talk in an interesting way and

be a good storyteller. You don't have to be an expert but at least make an effort to understand what it is that the media expects and even go as far as undergo training on how to come across confidently and as a professional.

3. Persistence – The journey is not an easy one and so you have to be and stay determined. I want you to stop and think about the number of authors and other amazing stories that come across the media daily. Do not ever think that you will be able to send out a media release and get contacted or invited for an interview straight away. You have to adopt the 'thorn in the side' approach. Bombard them with emails, telephone calls and focus your intention on getting onto their show. There are some that will interview you for a fee to help cover their running costs. Most people's opinion about this is split. However, if you were to ask me if I would do that, well the answer all depends on what is the asking fee and is it worth it? Do they have the audience to justify the fee? So, the main thing is, do not get easily downhearted or give up. This is an area where your WHY for writing the book comes into focus.

> **Persistence: The journey is not an easy one and so you have to be and stay determined**

4. Platform – This is where social media comes in to play. Use every social media platform that you possibly can. Facebook, Twitter, Instagram, LinkedIn, Snapchat and Pinterest. Let them become your new best friend or if you are already posting frequently on all these platforms, then

put them to good use. You will be surprised at the amount of attention and followers you can accumulate using social media.

As I mentioned earlier, you can start by simply stating that you are writing a book and also share what it will be about, thereon, you continue to trickle feed more onto the platforms.

Another step is to get a 3D Stack image done of your book cover so that you can start showing it off to the public and get people interested. Sharing excerpts from your book is another way to go about keeping the announcements going. If you have written an awesome bit of content or have covered a topic that could be controversial or is of high interest, then why not share a post about it or even do a short live video? This is an awesome option. Either do daily ones or set a specific date and time so that it is something that your audience will be expecting. You can ask questions, start a discussion etc. The main thing is to have a CTA (call to action).

Landing Page - This is a page that will be used as an entry point for your book and can also produce pre-orders via the landing page whilst building an email list.

Write blogs on topics surrounding your book and share tips that the reader can implement straight away as this will help gain credibility and build anticipation for the book.

Trending - Just like Forex, you need to follow the news and what is the topic of discussion. The moment that they are talking about a major topic, post about it, especially if it relates to your book. You may be wondering how effective this is? Well, when I wrote my first book, which addressed ADHD and the issues surrounding it, I was watching the early morning news one day and they were talking about Queen Elizabeth doing various visits that week concerning children with special needs. This prompted me to write to her and send her a copy of my book. I wasn't sure anything would come of it but did it anyway. I thought, 'what's the worst that could happen?' That decision earned me a letter of commendation from Her Majesty the Queen! You can also tweet about the topic along with an image of your book cover. This is also a good time to contact TV and radio stations as well as your local newspaper.

Volunteer - You can donate some time to do a talk about your book in various communities, organisations and groups, especially if it is something that is new to you.

These are just a few of the many things that you can do to drum up publicity around your book.

REVIEWS

Book reviews can be very helpful, though on the other hand, can also be discouraging and has the ability to determine the quantity of readers that will or won't purchase your book. Book reviews help potential readers become familiar with your book and give them some idea of if the book is what they are looking for and/or resonates with them. Some readers see reviews as a time saver and so if you have the ability to drum up some awesome reviews, it will then definitely work in your favour. A book review can enable your book to achieve greater visibility and help to amplify your book reach, even opening doors to new and greater audiences. The fact is that it's human nature for individuals to be curious about what's trending or popular and then want to check it out for themselves. A good number of book reviews can help lead to a huge impact on your book sales, however, DO NOT go down the road of inventing or outright buying book reviews. Think about it. Is it not a better feeling to see a great review posted about your book and know that somebody genuinely believes that your book is amazing in both content and value? I don't know about you, but I would be over the moon and I would definitely not get that feeling if I saw it knowing that I had paid to get someone to say something good about my book or even make it up myself, which is definitely not the same feeling.

Some of the following are ways that could help you to get reviews:

- Create a mailing list and ask your subscribers for reviews.
- Ask your friends, associates, colleagues, and family for reviews.
- Use marketing strategies like a book funnel to interact with the readers after purchase.
- Definitely follow-up messages – Be persistent. At some point they will do it just to get rid of you ha-ha (sounds bad but people are busy and writing a review, even though they may have loved your book, is not their main priority).
- Reach out to your followers and ask them to review your book.

- You can provide a free copy and ask readers to consider leaving a review. Let them know that there is no obligation to give a positive one as you want an honest review whether good or bad; both are acceptable.

- Use your social media platforms effectively and do CTA's (call to action). Put a direct link for them to click in order for them to leave a review as this makes the job a lot easier for them and always helps.

OFFER

Another awesome way of promoting your book is by offering giveaways. Some may say it's an underhand tactic, but it is not! Many large successful organisations thrive on offering giveaways. I will use an example. The likes of McDonald's and Burger King's Kids' Meals became famous not because it is the best tasting or a healthy food option for children, but just because of that little extra that they have added such as the box with all its trinkets and the magic of a free toy, right? Therefore, offering a little something special to your readers and target audience in order to build a buzz around your book is not harmful whatsoever. You need to get it out of your head that people are going to undervalue it because you have given it away. The main aim is that you are trying to catch their interest and then sell. You cannot sell to someone if you are not on their radar. One of my mentors, Andy Harrington, used this strategy with his book, I would like to share an example of an experience I had when my first book, 'Overcome and Rise Above,' was published. I produced rubber wristbands with the title of my book on it as a giveaway and applied an instruction.

Anyone wearing it when going through a challenging time during the day experiencing negative thoughts should pull the rubber band to snap their wrist. Yes, perhaps a little painful, but it would act as a reminder to them and return them to the state of, 'I can overcome and rise above.' (whatever the challenge was'). These were handed out at my book launch in goodie bags. I explained what they should do with it when giving my talk, and people seemed genuinely interested, and every now and then would send images of themselves wearing it to my Facebook page. About four months later I received a call from a man which really intrigued me, he had attended my launch and received one of the bands. He asked me if I had any more of the bands available to post to him. I said I had, and being a bit curious I asked him, 'do you love it that much?' The reply touched me. He said that he had been struggling with anger issues, and as a businessman, the triggers had been numerous and that the band had been helping him so much that it had now worn and snapped. I was absolutely gobsmacked and thrilled that something that I had given away had made such an impact and so I still offer them up until this very day and yes, he is still wearing them but not only that, he has forwarded many opportunities my way through connections and clients. You never know what it is that you will offer around your book that will make the world of difference to your reader and your business.

Another great and beneficial giveaway is that before the book is actually published, you offer a free chapter; this will build excitement about your book, help to build your mailing list, and at the same time be used as a presale tool.

Here is a list of some of the things that you can offer to your readers, obviously depending on what business or service you provide.

- A free 30 min consultation.
- Free evaluation.
- A gift (if you have another book or product that you can giveaway).
- Ticket to an event you may be having, i.e. book launch.
- Free chapter from the book.
- Downloadable version of your book.
- Online products.
- Promotional items (wristbands, pens etc).

These are just to name a few of the many things that you can offer. Put your brain to work and come up with ideas to make it unique and so start to think outside the box. The main aim is to create that buzz and build momentum.

MARKETING

Marketing a book is not as easy as it may seem, and a business book is not just about the book but should also have the concept of marketing your business behind it. There are so many factors and tips to look at and many of them go unused by authors. I was also one of them. The thing is, you cannot action what you do not know, right?

For a lot of new published authors, especially self-published, the biggest percentage normally comes from Amazon. However, the bigger sales happen on what you offer on the tail end, which is something we will be speaking about further on in this chapter. I mention it here because your marketing strategy needs to incorporate this fact and so there needs to be a clear plan to be executed. If you are going to mainly be using Amazon, then there are some handy tips that they offer which you need to take advantage of.

Using the right keywords - Keywords are used by various search engines such as Google and also Amazon. They enable the reader or client to understand what your book is about. Hence, ensuring that you have selected the right keywords is highly important, but they also need to be relevant. On Amazon you have the option of selecting seven keywords so choose them wisely. Using the right keywords is all about finding a specific keyword that will result in buyers using search queries to find your book on Amazon therefore making sure your book is discoverable.

Paperback and Kindle – In order to increase exposure, do both paperback and Kindle options. A little secret in this is that you can use different genre categories and also search words. I know many people aren't aware that they do not have to use the same keywords and categories for each version of their book. This will increase the chances of someone coming across your book. Amazon also allows you to have free book days, countdown deals, and Amazon Ads. If possible, I would encourage you to USE THEM!

AMAZON CENTRAL and AMAZON AUTHOR PAGE

Amazon Central:

There are a lot of authors that never setup an account on Amazon Author Central. There is a major disadvantage by not doing this.

What is Amazon Central and what does it do?

It's the platform that allows you to setup your author page on Amazon, which I will give more information on below, as well as:

- Adding the editorial reviews section for your book.
- Tracking your book sales.
- Seeing and responding to reviews.
- Engaging with your readers.
- Resolving any problems with your book listings.

Once you have a book on Amazon you have the ability to register for an Author Central Amazon account which will enable you to take advantage of creating your author page as you will definitely need one.

Amazon Author Page:

Amazon Author Page is your personal feature page on Amazon and access is enabled by getting onto Amazon's Kindle Direct Publishing. Using this platform will enable readers to learn more about you, the author, and see all your books. This will help in building fans, especially if you have written more than one book, as this will allow the possibility of grouping them together and getting them all in the view of readers. The Amazon Author page allows you to include the following:

- An interesting biography.
- A professional author photo(s).
- All of your books.
- Book trailers or other promotional videos.
- Feed to your blog posts.
- Follow button (+).
- Social media and website information.

You need to treat it like any other media platform that you have which engages with the public. Many do not have that either because they don't have the knowledge of it or recognise the relevance. You have to make the effort to take advantage of every available source of marketing because remember, it is not just about the book.

DIRECT MARKETING

Throughout the book I have mentioned the fact that all that you are doing should then lead to a larger process, such as a product launch, services or one that can create passive income such as a marketing funnel. This builds your authority and creates more revenue for you whilst giving your readers the opportunity to keep communicating with you and also opens the window for further sales and builds the ever-growing mailing list. If you are unsure of what a marketing funnel is, a friend of mine will be sharing a bit of his expertise with you on what it is and the benefits. It was cited in the New York Times that 'only a small fraction of self-published authors sells enough books to make a living, and many are put off by the drudge work and endless self-promotion involved.'

These are just a few steps that I have mentioned in regard to marketing but tend to be the ones that most authors never pay attention to. If you are willing to be amongst those who put in the work, then you stand in good stead when it comes to successfully marketing your book.

OUTSOURCE

The challenge you may come across as a new author is that you can get overwhelmed by all the actions you need to take, as trying to juggle everything whilst making sure you take the right steps may throw you off or not allow you to do as much to make your book hit its full potential. I would advise that you not get carried away by trying to do absolutely everything for free by doing it yourself; obviously do what you can, but there are some things that may pay off better and be more cost effective in the long run if you OUTSOURCE. Think about it. When you have very little knowledge or expertise in certain skills that are necessary for you to achieve publishing success, there is a high possibility that it will indeed show and reflect on your results for both you and your book. Do not be a one-man band and a 'know-it-all.' There is someone out there that knows something that you don't, and that might just be the thing that you need. Yes, you need to ensure that you tailor your budget to your pocket's ability, but also think of this as an investment into your business. I would advise that, to make it easier, you make a list of what needs to be done, make note of the ones that you honestly don't have the skill or know how to do, prioritise and then you outsource. This will enable you to not spend money unnecessarily, paying into and buying products and services that you may not have any use for immediately. This is an area where so many of us have fallen a victim by attending seminars or buying the golden carrots that you believe are going to miraculously turn your business into a money-making machine overnight, only to realise that you are not at the point where that product or service is needed for your business. Outsourcing the right way will help you to get more effective results and free up your time to work on what you do best.

Tail end – You may be wondering what I mean by this? As you know, with any type of marketing, there has to be an end goal in sight, the place that you are taking your clients to. You should have a clear plan of what comes next, what will be your next upsell or high-ticket product. I have mentioned previously that it's not the sale of the books that brings the money in but instead the product or service that you are going to sell. The book is only a positioning tool, using your content and an entry point to attract your ideal client; so now you have, is that the end of the road? If you have already written your book and you have not put anything in place well, I guess you now know why you haven't been making any money using your book. Possibly you have heard about or know about funnels, well this is where it comes in. I will share more about this in the next chapter.

ENGAGE

Begin drumming up interest in your book by engaging your audience throughout its development. Hint that you're up to something. Ask for their inputs on the cover design. Tease them with excerpts.

You'll also want to keep building your audience through blog tours, interviews, and media exposure. Try signing up as a source on Haro or SourceBottle.

Start working on your book launch at least six months in advance, because that's the minimum amount of time you need to start building relationships.

Get on the radar of influencers by supporting them and get yourself acquainted in groups that relate to your niche. If you have your own platform, like a podcast or blog, you can start to do videos around topics covered in your book and also, if possible, interview others that are known and relates to the topics you have covered in order to create awareness about your book and create a buzz.

When the time comes, send influencers copies of your book, and ask for an endorsement and/or a review. If they like the book enough, they may even promote it to their audiences.

You can certainly have a website, but a well-designed and regularly updated blog is by far the best means of effective book promotion after Amazon. Your blog posts, if well written, have the possibility to get indexed by Google, then hopefully a good proportion of your blog visitors will come to you organically. For book promotion, this works superbly, because it is how people discover you as an author, your books and what it is that you do.

Engage with your audience tips:

1. Build your author brand – This is where your USP (Unique Selling Point) is important. You need to be unique to your brand, your message and to your clients. This will also establish trust with your audience as they get to know who you are and what you stand for.

2. Become the authority figure – By delivering value at all times and being consistent in whatever it is that you are doing whether it be sending emails, doing blogs, YouTube videos or vlogs etc.

3. Begin to speak - Look out for speaking opportunities, book signings, readings, or as a presenter at a conference, as this adds credibility and exposure for your book.

4. Join networking events - Joining groups is pivotal in helping you attract speaking and promotional opportunities. As I mentioned, things really turned around for me when I joined the Professional Speakers Academy.

5. Create a workshop or seminar - Events will help you get known and also position you as an expert. If you have not yet done an event a great one to start with is your book launch.

Plan Your Launch

Once you have finished your book, the next logical step is the book launch. Essentially, a book launch is the promotional activity that introduces your book to the entire world.

Whatever your goals for publishing a book, the way you promote it needs to fit around them. For example, if you want to make it to the Amazon bestseller list, you have to aim to get copies of your book sold through Amazon and not bookshelf buyers, and you have to do it within a specific time. Your strategy could include an online launch day offering a bonus to people who order the book; you can also offer it at a discounted price or run a pre-order campaign as pre-orders will also count towards the first week of sales.

Create a landing page to get data so that you can start building a mailing list which will enable you to send out email information and build rapport with your audience as the more they warm to you, the more likely it is that they will then buy from you when you begin selling.

Starting a Facebook community is also a very effective way to engage with your audience by giving information, having discussions and giving your audience a chance to not only ask questions, but also get answers to many unanswered questions they may have. This will assist in building a tribe or raving fans that will help to promote you wherever they go and direct people to your launch.

Use social media effectively to promote your big day and build interest. Share excerpts do Facebook live promotions, Instagram, Twitter; basically, whatever platform is at your disposal. This is also where media release comes in handy as you want to also connect with the local newspapers, radio and TV stations. Do not limit yourself or think that they won't be interested – you are now an author so claim that place of authority and put yourself in the spotlight as you cannot expect someone else to do it for you if you are not willing to do it for yourself. The alternative is of course to pay for PR services to get it all done for you.

PLANNING FOR THE BIG DAY

A book launch does not have to be a physical event, it can also be an online launch. This does still require a lot of work to get done so please do not think it's the easier option as this can actually turn out to be even more difficult than doing a physical launch event as it is far different from getting individuals into a room where there may be food, entertainment and networking. An online launch though needs to be done effectively, which will allow you to get unlimited attention and can happen on a global scale, so it is indeed one thing to keep in mind. Here are some tips if you are planning to do an online launch.

PREPARE

PLAN

PROMOTE

PARTY

You need to create a massive buzz and media blitz. If possible, do a book tour. When you're launching your book on or offline, you need people to hear about your book in as many ways as possible.

- YouTube videos
- Twitter
- Facebook
- Instagram
- Pinterest
- Blogs
- Google+ posts and Hangouts
- Tumblr
- Podcasts
- Mailing lists

Create a media kit and have it ready at hand to share. What should this include?

- A short or long bio.
- High resolution photo(s).
- Links to your social media profiles..
- High resolution book covers
- A synopsis of your book.

Be prepared to do some hard work!

Offline Book Launch Planning

This also takes a lot of work but can be an enjoyable experience if planned well. Let me share the five things that I believe are a priority when planning a book launch event.

1. **Plan budget** - How much you want to spend is totally up to you, but this is where many tend to overspend. Therefore, keep in mind that a simple, well-planned launch can also be very effective without being too costly. The main spend should be focused on the following:

   - Hire cost of the venue.

   - Food/drinks for guests.

   - Printing of books to have available for signing.

   - Decorations.

   - Other promotional materials and prizes.

2. **Publicity** – By invitation only or public (also, will it be a free or paid for event?)
   The decision is completely yours, so if you are wondering how to make the choice then you need to just decide on whether:

   - You want a nice night to celebrate your book with family and friends, if so, then the option should be an invitation only event.

   - If you'd like to use your book launch as more of a means of promotion and getting it out there, then you should consider hosting a public event.

- You also need to keep in mind the fact that it would also be nice to have someone of interest attend. It could be for instance, your Mayor, Councillor or a celebrity. If this is the case, then you need to plan early and get their invite to them in time as they may have a busy schedule.

With regards to entry, will it be free or paid? Either one, a ticketed event will enable you to gain access to the name and email addresses of your attendees which will also contribute to your mailing lists, i.e Eventbrite

3. **Place** – Your venue needs to be nice, welcoming and at a central location that is easily accessible using public transportation. The types of venues commonly used are:

   - Bookstore and/or library.

   - Local café, bar or lounge.

   - Hotel.

   - Hired function room.

4. **Prepare** – To sell. (Ensure you have payment facilities in place and order forms. Never forget the tail end should still be kept in sight).

5. **To speak** – You have to give a speech and also share excerpts.

6. **To sign** – It's a special day for you and your book so be prepared to feel like a star on the day, and signing the book for your guests is part of the magical experience.

7. **People** – You need to remember that this is your day and so cannot do all of the tasks by yourself. YOU MUST DELEGATE!

   - To welcome guests.

   - To handle book sales.

   - Master of Ceremonies.

   - Waiters (if serving drinks /food).

   - Event organiser – (to ensure that everything is going to plan).

There are many more aspects to planning your big day, but I have shared with you the ones that need immediate attention and you can start to work on this before the book is even complete. So, grab a notebook and start writing down your ideas and creating a list.

CHAPTER SEVEN

How to Use Your Book as a Marketing Tool

In this chapter I will be sharing with you the various ways in which to use your book as a marketing tool as well as enabling you to see the impact becoming an author can have on your business through the stories of other authors I have come to know. At the beginning of my journey I didn't realise how becoming an author could make any difference to me in relation to my business, but oh wow was I wrong. The book not only created visibility for me, but it was through the content of my book that I was able to create and commence my coaching business which started to generate income. The possibilities and opportunities kept coming, and I was opened up to a new way of thinking and my business began to expand, but before this, I had the misconception that money would come from the book sales. However, I slowly came to the harsh reality that this was not the case. Ok, so let's get down to it and address the money-making side of things. These steps are the ones I took that helped me on my journey and if implemented, can also assist you in using your book as a successful marketing tool for your business.

AUTHORITY MARKETING

What is this and why does this matter? I mentioned in chapter one about the importance of being seen as the authority in your field. Authority marketing is the concept of marketing from a place of authority. Think about it. One of the things that gives clients the impulse to buy high ticket products is the perceived value – this is how much someone thinks you are worth, and being an author definitely enhances this. Not only this, but if you sell your book, this psychological act of paying for your authority, even if only a small purchase, makes it easier to sell more. It opens the door to larger purchases and doing further business with that person.

MAKE YOUR BOOK AN OPT-IN ON YOUR CONTENT

This strategy requires a lot of writing, but it is very effective. You need to create content that your audience wants to read. Embed a form that offers to email them your book for free. It can be a free downloadable copy or offer a paperback copy that whilst still free, a charge is made for postage and packaging. This will help to collect email addresses and build relationships enabling you to be able to upsell.

USE YOUR BOOK CONTENT TO CREATE WORKSHOPS

This is just one way to add an additional source of revenue for your business. You are literally going from becoming an author to expert and teacher. If done accurately your content can be changed into a highly successful workshop or online training course.

RE-PURPOSING YOUR BOOK CONTENT

Re-purposing your book content will enable you to have even more content, which is an awesome way to add extra streams of passive income to your business. The potential that can come from this is enormous. Think about it. Membership sites, Facebook communities, YouTube channel, online courses, SEO, all of which can be used to generate more traffic, which then means more customers.

SOCIAL MEDIA STRATEGIES

Utilising social media to promote your book and its content can really boost your visibility and your business.

- Post your experiences and each successful event that you have had with the book no matter how small.

- Write blogs from your book content (you don't have to reinvent the wheel).

- YouTube videos addressing the topics covered in your book.

- Crowdsource your book topics.

- Answer questions on Quora and become a source on Haro or SourceBottle.

LEAD MAGNET FOR PURCHASING FUNNEL

A purchasing funnel is a consumer-focused marketing model, which is a set of steps a visitor needs to go through before they can be converted to your high ticket products. The client converts from browsing to taking the action you want them to take. Your book will be the entry point to attract and pull your clients in therefore, you need to ensure that the content is indeed valuable. Have a look at the image below as an example.

As an author, it is up to you to determine how you are going to generate profit from your book. For some people, just becoming a published author and selling copies is enough. Most authors, however, are now earning some cash from their content and use it to create additional revenue. The long and short of it is that as an author, the two basic ways you can earn money from your book is by book sales or the services you sell based on your book's content.

JUDITH WRIGHT – MARKETING EXPERT

Here is some insight shared by an awesome friend of mine Judith Wright into the areas of marketing.

Judith Wright was born and bred in Yorkshire and is renowned for her no- nonsense, straight forward approach to life, and regularly entertains audiences about her 'journey' through life and business. Judith is an author, trainer, speaker and serial entrepreneur. She ran a marketing agency for over 18 years where she developed a proven five-part system for marketing that when followed, creates astounding results. She is currently involved in several businesses in the UK and Europe. Over the years she has worked with thousands of businesses to help them to articulate their vision and plan their journey to success. Amongst juggling her business interests, she is also a wife, mum, grandma and owner of two rescue dogs.

THE BOOK IS WRITTEN – WHAT COMES NEXT?

So, you've written your book, and you can now use it to position yourself as an expert, gain credibility, increase your visibility and stimulate sales.

Could you do me a favour? At this point, right now at the outset, before we go any further, I want you to write down a list of ten words that you would want people to say about you once they have spent some time in your company. If you really want to get the most out of this simple exercise, text ten people you know and ask them to say ten words to describe you. Do the sets of words match? Are there some that aren't there that you would like to see?

The results of this exercise will give you a great starting point to enable you to manage your own personal brand. The point is, as the author of this book you have written, you only have one chance to make a first impression. So, what will that first impression be? Whether that be in person or virtually, you need to create the same impact.

Are you full of energy and enthusiasm about your book? Do you look the part?

When people meet you, do they want to be like you? If they do, fantastic! If they don't you will be on an uphill struggle to sell your book. People need to walk away from any interaction feeling motivated to know more. When you are planning your marketing always keep that in mind.

So, before we get into the specifics, I'd like you to think about your book and who it is written for. If you get this element correct, you will have customers lining up to buy your book. If you get it wrong, the chances are you will be watching other author's book sales soar whilst yours isn't selling. So, what am I talking about? Well the first **M** in my proven marketing system stands for **Market**; not the supermarket or the fish market, but your target market, the people who will want to buy your book. You need to know and understand them in order to build a relationship with them that leads to them wanting to purchase your book. The answers to the following questions should help you to form all of the decisions you make about where you position yourself and the book.

Who will benefit from reading it?

Are they business owners/solopreneurs/entrepreneurs?

Are they employed? If so, what is their job role?

Are they male/female?

How old are they?

Where do they live?

Where do they work?

What do they read?

What do they listen to?

What do they do in their spare time?

Which social media channels do they use?

The clearer you are about who the potential buyers of the book are, the more you will be able to reach those people and convert them into customers. Once you know who they are, create a customer avatar so that all your communications are targeted accurately towards them. You may have several avatars at the end of this process. Here's an example of what one might look like.

- Marcus is self-employed and has his own office in London.
- He is 25-35.
- He reads professional publications online.
- He subscribes to personal development podcasts.
- He enjoys eating out and is a wine connoisseur.
- He uses Facebook and Instagram extensively.
- He likes expensive branded clothing.

So now you know who you are talking to we can move to our next M. When you get this right, your potential customers will hear your message above that of your competitors. If you get this wrong, they won't hear you and your message will be lost within the thousands of messages we all receive every day. Therefore, the next step is to craft your **Message**. To help you to do this you need to think about the pains your target market is facing. Once you understand this you can then focus on the solution your book is providing. The more you understand their pains the more your key messaging can demonstrate why reading this book will make their life a whole lot easier. The third step is to identify the **Media** you need to use to get those key messages into the ears of your target market. That is why your avatars are so important in order to guide you where to go. As an example, if your avatar is a 25-year-old female it is unlikely you would want to advertise on the radio, but you would certainly want to target her through Facebook! There is a whole host of ways to do this but let's keep it in three main categories:

Online

Offline

Others

Online – This means utilising your website and social media channels such as your Facebook page, Twitter, Instagram etc. The list goes on and on and will depend on your customer avatars. You can use your book to create content to share via blogs and/ or share snippets as excerpts. Create an audio version of the book so you can use a chapter to give away and help to build your list through the marketing funnels you have set up. You can reach out to other sites that have the same audience as you and offer to share content and create reciprocal links on your websites.

Find out who the bloggers are that cover your subject and develop a relationship with them. Send them the book to review and blog about. Consider if there are other businesses out there who could recommend your book and might be interested in putting an affiliate link on their website. Make sure you create an email signature which has information about the book and a link for more information and where to buy. Once you have built a list, make sure you adopt a 'keep in touch strategy' so that you can continue to build your relationships.

Offline – There are lots of opportunities for you to position yourself as an expert in your field and increase your visibility, and many people believe that once you have written a book around your subject, your status is massively elevated instantly. You may want to consider hosting a physical book launch, where people have the opportunity to buy the book and have it signed by you, the author. The local press may cover the event. It is always worth doing a press release and sending it off to the media that is relevant to your book topic. If you have an interesting photo to send with it, you usually have more chance of your piece being covered. Develop relationships with journalists. They love it when you make their life easier. Become known as someone who can act as a spokesperson on your chosen subject. Run a competition with them to win copies of your book. Identify relevant publications that relate to your subject area and do the same with them. This activity will no doubt be published online. In addition, most newspapers and magazines also have an online presence as well. Attend relevant networking events and offer to be the speaker. Make sure you get permission to use the business cards you collect and utilise the contact details to build your list. You may want to offer to go into local schools, maybe even the schools that you yourself attended. Every year they do book weeks and often feature local authors.

Others – Who do you know who can help you spread the word? Get a big piece of paper and create a brain dump of everyone you know; you may need several large pieces of paper!

Family.

Friends.

Work colleagues.

Business associates.

Groups you are involved with.

Connections from school.

Go through your phone contacts.

Facebook friends.

Who do you know who has a list of people they communicate with who would be interested in your book? Try to create a win-win situation so you can help them and in return, they will help you by sending your information out to their contacts.

Once you have selected your media you then need to think about the fourth M. You would never set off on a journey without planning how to get to your destination and creating sales for your book is just the same. You need to create a map. What do I mean by map? Well, what I mean is, you need to map out your journey and create a plan. They say if you fail to plan, you plan to fail. You won't be able to do everything at once so map it out and create a workable plan with timescales. There is a wealth of evidence to prove that people who have a plan achieve greater levels of success than those that don't. Consistency is key to getting results. It is doing the things on the plan that will mean results happen. I have seen too many people start off full of good intentions only to fail because they kept the intention but didn't take the necessary action to bring the intention into reality. It doesn't need to be a complicated plan, but it does have to be something you are committed to. Use it as an aid to trigger your actions.

The final step to look at is measure, and by that, I mean the measures you will put in place so you will know your efforts are paying off. How are you going to decide what you will measure? Book sales are an obvious measure, but you may well consider other things such as:

Number of unique visitors to your website.

Growth in social media channels (likes/follows/interactions etc).

Number of people on your list and speaking slots attended.

There is one thing I know to be true. Whatever we focus on improves and grows, so the more attention we pay to these measures the better results we will see. I would suggest you monitor the areas you have selected, ideally monthly but definitely every quarter. That way you can see any adjustments you might need to make within the plan and the action you are taking to get the results.

I hope this has given you an outline framework to help you to plan for your own success. I'd love to hear how you get on - drop me an email, I'd love to hear from you. I wish you every success and remember to enjoy the journey because the destination is merely the end.

If you want to know more, you can connect with Judith using the details below.

You can find out more about Judith at www.judithwright.co.uk or email her on hello@judithwright.co.uk

If you'd like to meet her go to www.meetjudithwright.com

Authors share their story and experience.

I have a few friends who have ventured on the author's journey, and I thought it would be great for them to share their stories with you on how becoming an author has transformed their life and business.

Claudia's Story

Have you ever aspired to achieve something you really wanted?

It's a cold day in April 1996. As the sun streamed through the window of a cramped public sector office with blank cream walls and the aroma of coffee in the air, there's low level chatter of probation officers and administrators. A younger me was sitting tense and nervous waiting for the phone to ring. One phone call was about to change my life forever.

The phone rang. 'Hello. Claudia here.'

'It's Geoff. We've offered it to someone else, Claudia. Sorry,' said a man's baritone, middle-class voice. 'On paper you were outstanding, that's why you were interviewed. But your performance wasn't that good. Actually, I expected much better.'

'But you know I can do that job, Geoff. You know that I've been helping the Probation Service develop equality and diversity for years'.

'Yes, and you've been great. But in the interview, you just didn't shine. Did you even prepare?'

Have you ever had a conversation like this with someone and you thought, maybe they're right?

I was devastated! My one chance to get that dream job and I'd blown it. And it's not as if these dream jobs come every day. Like buses, they're never there when you want them.

And that voice in my head kept saying 'You're not as good as they think you are, are you? You've been found out'. Geoff was right; I didn't prepare well. I thought this job had my name written on it. But I began to wonder 'what is the job for me?'

Have you ever had an experience that's completely pulled the rug from under you?

So time rolled by and opportunities came and went and I watched them pass me by, one by one. But after a while I found myself on the hunt for something that was right for me.

And if you'd been with me in July 1998, you would have seen me at a job fair in London Victoria, seated in a large, stately room with big windows with about fifty other people, 'all desperate too', I thought, as I listened to Curly Martin on stage.

And I'm looking at Curly Martin's rosy face and short, fair hair, which definitely wasn't curly. Little did I know what was about to happen. From the stage came, 'coaching is a powerful tool for helping people achieve their aspirations. And you can be a coach too. It can help people overcome their barriers, empower themselves and get what they want. The problem is that most people allow fear to stop them from realising their ambitions. Too many people, when things go wrong, step back when they should be stepping forward.'

'My God, it feels like she's speaking to me' I thought. That's exactly what happened to me. I got scared and withdrew'.

Coaching was something I knew I could do and enjoy. I'd been developing and supervising women for a long time. I'd managed teams really well. I'd trained as a therapist. I knew I could do this but was very fearful and allowed myself to get distracted with other things.

However, two years later, when I was given redundancy notice, I was well prepared. I'd trained to be a coach and was ready to take my redundancy pay-off and invest in my own business.

In March 2010, I set up Winning Pathways Coaching, and started doing what I love, in a way I'd not envisaged. I'm now an executive coach and a career coach and mentor, enabling women in the UK and abroad to step into their power. In the process I promote equality and diversity, particularly in relation to gender and race. In addition, since that time, I've coached many women working in organisations and in their own business. I've gained NLP and Master Coach Accreditations, developed as a public speaker and was nominated for Mentor of the Year twice by City, University of London before receiving the award in 2017. In 2018, I was nominated once again. I've also become an author three times. The first two books, both Amazon best-sellers, 'Winning in Life and Work' (2012) and 'The Power of Being a Woman (2015) were co-written. My third book, 'Ordinary Women Doing Extraordinary Things: 5 Steps to Add Extra to Ordinary', was a solo piece of work. It's a practical, action- focused step by step guide for women in the first few years of their careers who want to succeed. Individual stories of thirteen phenomenal 'page one women,' who have overcome diverse challenges and have been successful, and sources of inspiration.

Here's what I found about the process of writing a book. Commitment, organisation, planning and focus are key. For me it was hard work, and at times I was ready to give up, particularly when words wouldn't flow and my imagination wouldn't imagine. And yet there were times when it was all so easy and I couldn't stop writing. Attending writing weekends gave me much needed support and structure. And having a coach to hold me to account and boost my flagging energy was invaluable. Here's what I found about becoming an author. It's been a great confidence booster and brilliant for my personal credibility. People seem to admire me more and see me from a different perspective – as if I'm now cooler and smarter and more of an expert in my field. I've earned the attention of people who may not have been listening so intently previously. Opportunities to speak at events and sit on panels have increased. It's been great for my business. When I started to shout about my book at networking events the number of potential clients and leads increased. I've not made a profit from sales of my book, which isn't unusual - not many authors do, as the profit has come from the services I offer. However, I didn't write with an eye on the bottom line I wrote it to get my 'page one women' out into the world in order to inspire more everyday women into doing what they need to do to succeed. The book was an additional way of achieving my purpose to enable women to make a bigger contribution in the world and it also brought personal fulfilment. But here are a couple of important factors to note. To get the most from being an author, writing a good

> **Remember, those who succeed dream, plan and take action**

quality book is crucial. And by 'good quality' I mean one that has something to say, contains good ideas, gives a lot of value and is well written. Without these points you're putting your personal and business credibility at risk.

So, are you ready to achieve your ambition to write your book or get that dream role? Or are you willing to merely dream about it, talk about it and do nothing about?

Remember, those who succeed dream, plan and take action

Leila's Story

One cold afternoon in November 2000, you would have seen me sitting in a quiet meeting room, positioned in the middle of a large, bright, open-plan office. Across the desk is my boss, a super intelligent Cambridge graduate, quiet, reserved, and quite simply a great boss to work for! "Leila, I want to congratulate you on your top rating in this latest appraisal. It's a tremendous achievement…" As I slid the white envelope across the table to Peter… "Thank you Peter, it really means a lot, and it's been a privilege to learn from you…"

"Oh what's this? Surely not what I am thinking…" (Opens the envelope) "You're resigning? Is it the money? Have you been offered something else? I can look into that, see what we can do…"

"Actually, no. I don't want to work in finance anymore Peter. I want to become a recruitment consultant…It's not about the money…in fact I am taking a 50% pay-cut to move into recruitment"

"50%??? But you're in the process of closing on your new home. How will you afford the mortgage with such a huge drop in salary? Have you really thought this through Leila?"

You can probably tell Peter is a little risk-averse!

"Peter, it's fine. I have faith that it will all work out. It's a huge change for me, amassive risk I am taking I agree. But I need to follow my instincts, and just make the leap!" You see, I had done my due diligence on recruitment consultants, and I would love to do what they did! I want to be one of the good ones, one who really delivers value to my clients.

Back in the late '90's, I had realized my then dream of qualifying as a chartered accountant with the ACCA, and had the opportunity to build my breadth of finance experience in a range of diverse roles with some global organisations.

I received many negative comments from family, friends and colleagues. People thought I was crazy, having studied so hard to qualify and now their view was that I was throwing it all away for what was essentially a sales role!

Have you ever found yourself drawn towards taking action, doing something different, yet you find that a little voice inside your head, or indeed people around you, react negatively, question and challenge you, and maybe tell you you're crazy, that you can never do that? And maybe then you start to doubt yourself…Having taken that leap of faith…Then on Wednesday 3rd Jan 2001, suited and booted, I arrive at the offices of my new employer, a small recruitment firm in North London.

My director, Steve with super spiky hair and a big smile, greets me at the door, and shakes my hand enthusiastically; "Welcome to the team Leila, grab a coffee and I'll introduce you to the others. Then we'll start you off with a few cold calls to prospective clients – you'll promote the CV of our latest A-star candidate. Let's see how you get on…"

It was at this point that I panicked, and the little voice inside my head started…"what the hell! In front of this experienced team, I have to make cold calls, they will all be listening to me, what if I say something stupid, what if I mess up, what if I embarrass myself, what if…??? Oh My Gosh what HAVE I signed up to..???"

Irrational thoughts were flying through my mind, as the reality dawned on me. I had signed up to this. "Were the others right? Had I been crazy to make this giant leap into the unknown? It felt uncomfortable…but you know, 'stepping out of your comfort zone, is your biggest opportunity for growth.' I knew deep down I was doing the right thing, and that this was a job I could do, and love. And I remembered a quote I had read some years back by Jack Canfield… "By taking a leap of faith in the face of fear, you can transform your life" … so I sat down and picked up the phone…

Do you sometimes doubt your abilities, question whether you will succeed, or worry what others will think if you were to step out of your comfort zone?

Well, that's what I was thinking as I completed my first year in recruitment, and now it's time for my annual review with spiky haired Steve. He's still smiling: "Leila, I am really pleased with your performance this year. We took a risk on you, you had no real sales experience, yet you have done remarkably well. In fact, you have been our highest biller this year."

As I sat there, smiling at Steve, for me, it wasn't just about matching people to roles. It was also about encouraging people's beliefs in themselves, to get over their hurdles, make those leaps. Because many of them had to believe they were good enough in order to grab new opportunities!

My two years spent in recruitment, a huge step outside my comfort zone, remain perhaps the most profound and impactful time during my career, that enabled me to grow and transform professionally.

Fast forward to today, and for the last sixteen years I have had the good fortune to work for one of the leading global IT companies where I've combined my sales, finance and people skills in different ways, initially in corporate finance, and in the most recent years as a sales executive.

During those sixteen years, alongside my successful and enjoyable career, I have also mentored and coached many employees at various stages in their career, both on professional and personal matters.

In 2013, when my mum passed away, I found myself questioning my own life purpose, and whether working in the corporate world was something I wanted to continue for the rest of my life. Whilst I enjoyed my career, I knew I wanted something more! As Steve Jobs said: "Your time is limited, so don't waste it living someone else's life. ... have the courage to follow your heart and intuition. They somehow already know what you truly want to become. Everything else is secondary."

I began to actively pursue my personal development journey, investing significant time, energy and funds into my own personal growth, transformation and learning. As a consequence, over the last five years, I qualified as an accredited master coach (IIC and M), graduated from Anthony Robbins Mastery University and Business Mastery University, became a member of the Professional Speakers Academy (PSA) and an accredited speaker, coach, and a Master Practitioner of NLP and Hypnotherapy (ABNLP and ABH). I also received accreditation from Hewlett Packard Enterprise Learning and Professional Development as a trainer/facilitator, delivering both virtual and face to face training.

I quickly realized that in order to establish credibility and be seen as an authority in my field and build a business, I would need to write a book.

Applying my learning from the PSA and working with a book mentor, I created the system the 'Ultimate Success Blueprint™' and shared this system in my award winning book, "Success Redefined – How to leverage Your Natural Talents to Become Limitless!"

I rapidly began growing and establishing my transformational coaching business, empowering driven and highly motivated career professionals to discover their own definition of success, to realise their true potential and achieve their desired outcomes.

The publishing of my book in September 2015 has created numerous opportunities and opened multiple doors for me! It began with my first talk in Milan, Italy, followed by delivering a series of webinars sharing my system to a couple of global organisations, and ultimately creating opportunities to deliver inspiring, motivational, thought-provoking talks and workshops at various events and organisations including Hewlett Packard Enterprise, DXC, IBM, 3M, Dow Jones, Santander, Birkbeck University of London, Oxford Brookes University, multiple CIMA events with the pinnacle being the Women of Silicon Roundabout event held at the Excel in London. My book acts as my business card, especially when I meet with organisations. They love to see something tangible, and the system detailed in the book provides just that. I coach clients from early career starters through to executives, with a focus on going beyond surface level coaching, and drilling down to get to the root cause of any limitations, challenges and limiting beliefs, ensuring that my clients experience real and lasting transformation. In addition, I am a speaker trainer, applying my unique system, 'The Presenter Principles™' to mentor those wishing to create a powerful presence when speaking and presenting to an audience. I host regular webinars, write inspiring articles, and I am invited to speak at events and deliver workshops and training to share my powerful and thought-provoking philosophies.

> **I truly believe that having my book in hand positions me as an authority against potential competitors**

I truly believe that having my book in hand positions me as an authority against potential competitors, is a great conversation starter and opens many doors and opportunities. Whilst it is becoming commonplace in the entrepreneurial world to have a published book, this is not the case in the corporate world and as such stands out and creates a positive impression amongst potential clients. I am now an award-winning author, accredited coach, international speaker, speaker trainer, The Authentic Leadership Coach™, and Founder of The Authentic Leadership Academy™.

Leila Singh

Tel: +44 7956 199874

Email: Leila@leilasingh.com

www.leilasingh.com

https://www.linkedin.com/in/leila-singh/

Cheryl's Story

Stories have always been something I loved as a child – my parents worked a lot and so bedtime stories are a reminder of those precious moments of attention from them. Little did I know back then (nearly fifty years ago) how much stories would become part of my life. I see now looking back that from the age of five to forty-eight I was collecting stories of my life experiences that I would share in the second half of my life (yes, I am planning on living to at least ninety-six!!) And the best way to do this I have found has been through video and stage, to entertain in the moment and for a way, to be in someone's mind and to help to transform them in a way that can stay with them as a support; there is of course, a book.

Before I wrote my first book 'The Devil, the Angel and You,' I was afraid that I didn't know enough; maybe you know that feeling too? Well, here's the thing you only need to be one step ahead of someone else to help them and since this first book I have now been able to share what I've learned in order to help others to get away from their pain or indeed avoid it completely.

I feel very blessed to have won an award for the book I wrote in collaboration with Marion Bevington – 'Find Your WHY to Become Frickin' Awesome,' and to have achieved the number one best seller spot in countries including the USA, Germany, Holland and number two in the UK for '38 Transformational Lessons,' written with fellow board of directors (including Marie Diamond from the Secret) and members of The Association of Leaders (Europe).

Writing a book immediately gives you authority (I guess the clue is in the name!) and it helps you to help others. We have since then created a Facebook community which brings in a streamline of passive income. I have graced the stage as well as run retreats in various different countries. Whether you want to write a book on your own or in collaboration with others, my advice is just do it. A book will outlive you and will continue to help others long after you have left this planet and so what are you waiting for … start writing your legacy now

James Dewane

On a dreary, wet October day in 2007 you and I are aimlessly wandering the streets of Bromley. I am in a complete daze and literally have no idea which way to turn and you have no idea how to help me. I turn to you in utter desperation.

"What do I do now!? Where do I go!?"

You try to reassure me but I continue in my despair.

"My wife and I have got a baby on the way and we've just committed to buying our new home in Kent, and now I don't even have the bus fare home! How did this happen? I've just come out of a meeting with my friend Rob. I've known him for almost three years and I thought he was going to advise me how I get through this situation. He was supposed to help me! Instead I have come away with nothing, literally nothing!"

Rob is a financial adviser who specialises in helping companies who find themselves in trouble and I had just walked out of the office of my friend - who had just become my liquidator. He told me that due to the financial state of my company, I could not legally trade anymore, not for one more second. So, I could no longer trade, and I had to tell my staff that I had nothing left and I could not pay them. I was declared insolvent! I would also have to explain to my wife that our plans for a new home were in jeopardy. I felt a complete failure.

This morning I was a businessman, I had a thriving company, and employed nine staff, had three vans and a car on the road plus a nice little shop front office in South London. Now I had nothing; no business. In effect I was unemployed, my vans and car were company property so I couldn't use them nor could I access my company bank accounts. Even so, I was determined I was not about to become bankrupt. I had lost my business and had no idea how I was going to avoid personal bankruptcy, especially as I had borrowed heavily and just committed to a mortgage on a new house. I owed a lot of money and all I had now was my hand tools! Friends and family had helped me financially when I was building the business and the bank had trusted me with personal and business loans; any one of them could have pushed the bankruptcy button by forcing a repayment, meaning the new house and car and even the shirt off my back would have been gone and I could easily have been declared bankrupt, but, I managed to convince everyone to have some further faith in me and thankfully they did! Now I had to dig really deep and start again. After many trials and errors, I realised that it was not about giving up but trying new strategies.

"My challenges became my obsession and my obsession became my passion"... and as a result I studied everything I could about marketing and in particular local marketing. There was nothing out there for tradesmen so I looked at other sectors and figured out how to adapt marketing tactics and techniques used in those sectors and make them effective for me as an electrician. I attended workshops, went on short courses, weekend seminars, read books and bought audio and

> After many trials and errors, I realised that it was not about giving up but trying new strategies.

video programs. I also studied hypnosis and basic NLP (Neuro Linguistic Programming) and as my business grew, I joined mastermind groups and subscribed to newsletters and magazines from marketing experts in the US and the UK. In truth I spent a small fortune learning what works, but more importantly what doesn't.

A few years into my recovery, the period where I was working my butt off to claw my way back to success, I was involved with BNI (Business Network International). I joined a program ran by a guy called Andy Harrington and attended many meetings, learning how to package and deliver training. I studied public speaking and coaching and also became a member of the Association of Professional Coaches, Trainers and Consultants (APCTC). It was at this stage in the journey that I built what is now a very successful membership program - My Electricians ToolBox™.

My Electricians ToolBox™ is the only resource like it in the UK. It is where I house all of my training on marketing for tradesmen. It has tools, software training, downloads and help sheets… everything a tradesman or woman could need to market their business locally. Today we have members from not only the UK but also Ireland and as far away as Canada, the US and even Australia; all using and benefiting from this vast resource.

With Andy's help I also put together the program of practical workshops that I now run across the UK and Ireland. You can get details about these on www.jdewane.com/live.

Then he suggested I should write a book!

No surprise that I had the same old doubts pop up, but they were short lived, and I figured why not? Therefore, I wrote my book The S.P.A.R.K.S Blueprint™ to Marketing for Local Trades. The book became a number one best seller on Amazon after three weeks of being published and was top one-hundred for three years which was based on a strategy used to help me get it there.

This has helped me:

- Open doors to me becoming a guest in vlogs.
- I have also been recognised by the biggest association in the industry, NICEIC. They have a membership of over thirty-three thousand electricians in the UK and I now speak at all their national events twice per year and I am currently in the process of arranging training services.

- The book is now used as a lead magnet to a membership site which generates a residual income of six figures per year.

- It is now also a teaching tool for my potential clients as the content help them to realise the need to work with me.

- To add a uniqueness about what I do – as like you, I went against the norm of what electricians believe and normally do.

From my experience and knowledge gained I have also created a formula that will assist authors in becoming a bestseller – 'The Guaranteed Best Seller Strategy.'

Writing a book opens doors so do not underestimate or limit the power of becoming an author.

Deenita Pattni

Books!

A medium created to escape, elevate, educate and enhance. The words on a page constructed in a way that ignites your inner inspiration, intuition and imagination.

These are all important marketing traits that every business owner, entrepreneur and author must extract and elicit in order to reach their client base.

That's the marketing genius a book has when used in your business to position you as the expert in what you do.

That's what it did for me…

Has there been a time in your life where you have a love for something and you just can't explain it…

Come back with me…back to 1980. I am eight years old and it has only been a year since our family had moved from our flat in Kensington to our home in Harrow. I'm in my school; Elm Grove First School and I get called to the front of the classroom by my teacher…Mr Johnson. As I slowly walk towards him, the classroom feels really quiet! They're all listening. Am I going to get told off? Have I done something wrong? I want my mum!

As I looked up at Mr Johnson, his thin, long face and floppy ginger hair, I saw a smile on his face. "Deenita. Well done, you are now a free reader. That's brilliant and you're the first one in the class to get this! Very proud of you and keep reading!"

Initially confused, I soon discovered that being a free reader meant I had read all the books that were compulsory in the National Curriculum and now I could go to the library and choose to read any book I wanted, any time!

I chose….Charlotte's Web and it's still a book that makes me smile today!

That's the power of a book when you're a child; as mentioned earlier it ignites your imagination and insight and lets you think… **<u>Anything is Possible</u>**.

Therefore, the question in your mind may be; 'How does this relate to writing a business book?'

The first business book I read was 'Who Moved My Cheese' and a few hours later, I had resigned from a job which was making me extremely miserable without another job to go to! When I first started my business in 2012, having been made redundant with no backup plan, I read my next business book, 'Rich Dad, Poor Dad,' and I am still in business today!

For me, I realised that when reading a well written, well laid out business book, it had the ability to motivate me; keep me on track; evolve my knowledge and apply it on my business; be inspired; work more effectively and changed my relationship and mindset around money. More importantly – the books I read simply made me do one thing and more of it – take action!

ACTION

In 2012, I started my training and development business; having qualified as an NLP Trainer and worked in recruitment for seventeen years. I had inserted a training element into my role where I took time out to train members of the team resulting in them creating better results because of adopting a better mindset so when I started Viamii Training Academy, the decision to transition my career into training and development was an easy one. And given my previous successes, to offer myself out as a recruitment trainer was a no brainer.

However, a couple of years in there was just one major problem! I lived in London and there was a recruitment trainer on every street corner! The market was saturated with professionals claiming to be the best in their field. Now I'm not saying they weren't great but I did ask myself the question…how could I stand out from this sea of sameness?

In 2014, I found myself in a seminar room and in front of me was a hugely animated speaker who was sharing his knowledge and knowhow on how writing a book was the key to being seen as the expert in your industry. A book was what replaced your business card. When someone asked 'do you have a business card?' you would be able to respond; 'No, but I have a book,' and the response back would be nothing less than, WOW!

I knew from that moment that that would make a huge difference! And the decision was made. I would write a book!

Having read a number of interesting business books; I knew I wanted mine to leave no stone unturned. I wanted to inspire through education and share my big WHY. I wanted recruitment professionals to feel connected and relate to me and feel the way I did when I read a book…**Anything is Possible!**

I created a framework of my service by offering and writing the chapters based on this framework, giving tips and techniques throughout so every reader would receive value. I got illustrations, a book cover designed with my brand colours and testimonials from past clients to put on the back! And even reached out to my target market on LinkedIn to give their opinion on the best book title!

<u>Recruitment Gems Uncovered</u> was born!

Now it was time to use this gem as a marketing tool! 'Recruitment Gems Uncovered' was used in a number of ways to get my name and brand out there to my target market! Initially, the usual posts on social media. From the moment I received the first delivery, pictures were taken and posted on LinkedIn, Facebook and Twitter. The book cover made it onto my cover and background pictures on my social media platforms.

A sales funnel was created so I could give away my first chapter for free as a lead magnet; every training client got free copies for their staff in return for a testimonial. Every event I ran, the book would be at the back of the room on sale. Before I knew it, my fans (the small amount there were) started to recommend me as a recruitment trainer and my introduction to prospective clients had a different impact when I started with "I'm the published author of Recruitment Gems Uncovered…"

And then I received this…

Excellent read for any coaches out there in recruitment. Was gifted this book just before a final interview and just after reading the first few pages I knew I would get the job! Inspiring and motivating in a very simple understandable way. I keep the book by my desk at work and share pages with my colleagues. Will be looking out for future events.

My first review; a recruitment professional who contacted me on LinkedIn to thank me!

It felt like my book had done just what I intended it to. Made someone feel inspired and get results!

Therefore, the question was; how could I get more of the same and help more people!

That's when I knew I had to drive the marketing forward more and also give myself a new title! That of 'Amazon Number One Best Seller.'

Therefore, with a little bit of help from my marketing friends we launched a campaign on Amazon to get the book to the number one spot (in paperback). We reduced the book, for a limited time, to £1.99 and started sharing this by promoting it and creating lot of noise about it on LinkedIn, Facebook and Twitter as well as Instagram!

The campaign started at 11pm on Friday 13th September 2018 and the deadline was to get it to the number one by 1pm the next day! By 12.45pm, 'Recruitment Gems Uncovered' got top spot in HR Training!

And this led to me winning Author of the Year 2019. Now I was an award-winning Amazon Number One Best Selling Author.

This led to a second award in 2019 by the Brand Builders Club – a global branding training company whose award sponsors recognized the books that had impacted lives!

'Recruitment Gems Uncovered' not only helped me gain more clients and credibility within my industry but also on a wider scale as an entrepreneur. I received recognition and was approached to contribute in other publications regardless of industry.

I also co-authored the first volume of 'Pay It Forward: Notes to My Younger Self' where along with 17 other women I shared my own personal journey so I could inspire others to feel…**Anything is Possible!**

My business then took a turn. Having evolved my knowledge and know-how, I began to focus more on another area of my business, an area which I had been dabbling in because people asked me to help them with it. But now, the demand in this area was increasing and so it became my main focus.

I transitioned once again from training recruiters towards now training entrepreneurs, small business owners, coaches, authors, trainers, consultants and solopreneurs on marketing themselves on LinkedIn, a powerful platform, and helped them turn their connections into paying clients!

But after all the hard work I had made towards becoming the 'go to' expert in recruitment training, I was afraid of letting go so I was splitting my time trying to build two businesses areas! I found myself having coffee with my mentor, Andy.

Andy: "Why are you still focusing on the recruitment side? LinkedIn is where it's at and you're amazing at it. So focus on that and build that! The recruitment is the old you! Let go"

Me: "I know but what about everything I've done! I've written a book on recruitment training!!! I'm a published author in this area!"

Andy: "So??? Write another book! It's about time"

'LinkedIn Gems Uncovered'…here I come!

Ben Green

My name is Ben Green and I am a dedicated child practitioner (BSc/JNC), wellbeing coach, fitness professional, the founder and director of Activ8 Fitness Cam and author of "A STEP TO ACTIV8TION Volume 1"

Since the age of sixteen I have been committed to the vision of making a positive change in society and empowering every child I work with. In 2014 I founded the innovative company 'Activ8 Fitness Camp' with a mission to 'inspire and motivate our future generations by 'Activ8ting' their inner greatness'. Over the years my journey has included supporting hundreds of children and families through using different approaches to enhance a positive wellbeing, particularly through fitness training, nutritional workshops and specialised 1:1 life coaching sessions. Ben has worked in a wide range of educational settings including nurseries, primary schools, secondary schools, alternative education, specialised schools (autism spectrum disorder/ social, emotion and mental health conditions) and secure units. I have gone on to driving the company forward to many successes. Activ8 Fitness Camp was awarded the community organisation award at the National Diversity Awards 2017 and also shortlisted at the Heathrow European Diversity Awards 2017.

My journey to becoming an author began when meeting Michelle at a motivational event in London. We happened to be sitting on the same table and connected almost immediately. We exchanged business cards, and this is when the magic started. Michelle made the entire process a dream. I presented Michelle with my book idea and I could tell this resonated with her. At this point Michelle discussed with me how this book could support her own children. For me, this was the first time I had shared my idea to someone outside of my personal circle and the feedback I received from Michelle was honest and a massive eye opener to the potential impact my book could have. The plan of action was created, from regular meetings, book launch planning, media, social media promotion, book sales strategy meeting; you name it, Michelle had it covered.

Since 'A Step to Activ8tion Volume 1' has been published, my company (Activ8 Fitness Camp) have used this book as a tool in education and community settings. We have facilitated a number of theory and practical workshops using the book as a structured programme.

I have been invited to read my book in a number of community centres to inspire the future generations to take control of their own wellbeing and also received media coverage as I was featured in an interview on Sky TV. It has been an amazing journey and the success derived from becoming an author has propelled me to writing more series which are coming soon, so if you are after visibility and becoming an authority in your field, then writing your book is the way to go.

I hope that the content and these amazing stories has shed some light to the many things that becoming an author can open you up to. Here is the thing; gone are the days when you had to have the best grammar, speak fluent English or have the largest vocabulary in order to write a book. You just need to know your content, know your client and get the information you need in order to achieve success; the professionals are available to handle the rest.

One major thing I came to recognise on my journey that made the significant shift for me is a skill that many want, and that is to have the ability to do, and to be honest, that is one of the main reasons that most of my clients give as one of the WHY's for them writing their book; to become a speaker. Here's the thing, the book world is becoming saturated and so you need to bring attention to your book and become notable. You cannot remain reserved and have the 'I don't want to be in the spotlight' attitude, which is not good for your marketing. Becoming a speaker *enables you to garner attention for your book and to get away from that mindset.* The fact that you don't consider yourself to be a great speaker does not mean you cannot learn the skills you need.

As I mentioned in my story, I took the leap and invested in Andy Harrington's Professional Speakers Academy where I learnt the art of becoming a professional speaker and how to use the authority that I now had from writing my book to becoming a visible authority and expert in my field. Here's the thing; an unknown author with a book having zero shelf development and filling boxes in the loft is no authority at all; you have to go out there and show yourself as the authority and the greatest way to do that is to become a speaker; this will then lead you to what Andy Harrington calls the 'Micro Celebrity.'

I took the liberty of speaking with the man himself. 'Mr. H' as is often called, to get his expert advice and insight into book writing and becoming a speaker.

SO WHO IS ANDY HARRINGTON?

Andy was in 1969 in London. He now lives in Kent with his wife Beckie and his five children Josh, Tom, Gemma, Amelia and Alfie.

At age twenty-nine, Andy was working in a call centre for an insurance company making just £1500 per month. Frustrated with his dead end job he borrowed £10,000 from the bank and started a business that has now pulled in more than £50,000,000 ($78,000,000) in revenue. Since selling his company, Andy has gone on to coach Hollywood movie stars and some of the world's best speakers through his Public Speakers University and Professional Speakers Academy and hosted major life changing events such as 'Power to Achieve,' 'Stand and Deliver,' 'Passion into Profit' and 'Millionaire Mentors.' He has shared the stage with Sir Richard Branson, Anthony Robbins, Sir Alan Sugar, Brian Tracy, Paul McKenna and Bob Proctor of 'The Secret', to name but a few.'

Andy's passion is in raising peoples earning potential by breaking them out of the limited mindset of how much they think they are worth. His Power to Achieve Weekend Seminar has helped improve the quality of lives of thousands of successful people around the world and is a must attend for anyone serious about realising their potential. He has been invited to speak at the world's most prestigious venues in Australia, Dubai, Malaysia, Singapore and London, including Wembley and the biggest indoor venue in Europe, The London O2 Arena, where he captivated an audience of over 8,500 people.

They laughed at me when I said I was to going to set up my own business

Andy enjoys spending holiday time with his wife and children or watching them dance or play sport. He is a keen cricketer having played for Kent at U19 level. He also loves football having played for Gravesham District and Kent County.

"They laughed at me when I said I was to going to set up my own business but when I became a Sunday Times Best Selling Author, shared the stage with Tony Robbins, Bill Clinton and Donald Trump they all wanted to know how I did it!

THE INTERVIEW

Me: So, Andy, you are a Sunday Times Bestselling Author of the book 'Passion into Profit.' What challenges did you have writing this book?

Andy: Really, it was about deciding what the book was actually because in reality, business books don't sell as well as most novels right? So, you've got to get the title right, and what the book is about has to have enough wide appeal. I didn't know how to narrow it so that it appealed to a number of people, and that was the biggest challenge.

Me: Great, that's a challenge many upcoming authors have, which is how to target their niche and stay with the primary objective of keeping their ideal client in mind at all times. Andy, what was the reason, or as I call it, the WHY behind writing your book?

Andy: Two things for me really. One was a bit of vanity, in that I really wanted to be a published author and also become a Sunday Times bestselling published author, which is the reason why I went down the published route rather than the self-published route. The second one obviously was to use it as a lead generation tool to pull more people into what I do. Obviously in hindsight, you know if I did it again, I'm not entirely convinced I would go down the published route because I guess I've got the visibility now so I probably would go for the more controlled option, which would mean that when using it as a lead generator, I wouldn't have to buy the books off my publisher to put them into my funnel, which is a more expensive way of going about it.

Me: Great stuff, so how long did it take you to write the book?

Andy: It took me about thirty-six to fifty hours of actual writing, though not all at the same time obviously. Now, if I probably spread it out, it was over a three month period.

Me: That is awesome. So tell me, how did you go about getting the content for your book in that short space of time?

Andy: The content was really generated from a template, model or framework if you like, which I already had. It is a recipe for how I do what I do. I'm obviously teaching people how to create the content for their business, which is what you are also modelling yourself with your project of showing them then how to turn that content into a book. It was just the case of making sure that I made the language accessible. I wanted to make it a really easy read because it's not really about teaching per se, although obviously it is a how-to book. It is the opening isn't it, so in one term, we don't want to make it too complex. I wanted to make it something that people could read, you know on a journey from London to Manchester, on an airplane journey or probably a train to be fair, and then back again.

Me: Has the book made any difference or impact to your business?

Andy: Yes, I do believe it has. Writing a book does up your status. With every video I do, I can say 'Andy Harrington, the Sunday Times best-selling author,' so it's something, it's a status stamp and has opened a few doors but probably as well, just a sense of fulfilment of completion and belief in yourself. You know because once you are a published author, that's another validation isn't it; that maybe you are somebody of, you know, some worth, and that maybe, also other people might be more interested in what you have to say, especially as a speaker and authority figure, so yeah, for sure, definitely it has made an impact. I think I'd also say it's probably inspired other people to also therefore write their book because they might look at it as being more possible a step for them to take right now.

Me: You mentioned that you used your book as a lead magnet, so do you want to explain that process a bit more about how you did that?

Andy: So I've used a few different strategies. The initial one we used was the free book plus shipping strategy. Even though the book was retailing at ten pounds ninety-nine, I bought from the publisher for a couple of pounds, and what we then did was in essence, clients got a chance to obtain the book for free, they just paid for the shipping which was four pounds ninety-nine. This actually covered the cost of the two pounds I paid for the book from my publisher plus the shipping to them so I was able to break-even at least on the sale. It doesn't mean that it covered the cost of the advertising just the cost of the book, but then once they said yes or opt-in for the book, we would then offer a second offer on the confirmation or thank you page where an upsell is added plus an extra bonus on top of the product so that when enough people purchased it that would then cover the cost of the advertising so it would make us a profit. However, the motive is not just about making a profit at this stage, but more the fact that

I've just acquired a customer now completely free, and because it's got so many other things I can offer them on their journey, such as attending my live events, join my mastermind programs, academies etc, which are as you know in the two thousand pound range, there's a much higher probability that they will actually purchase those whether immediately or sometime later on. Book sales profits is not where the money is unless you're lucky enough to be one of those authors who sells millions for example J.K. Rowling; unfortunately, most business books don't. So, if you can break even and secure a customer and they can consume the content in the book that you've written, then that's great. With the book it's almost like you are speaking to them isn't it, so that little Trojan horse of the book will do the magic and work for you, to position you as an expert, adding value, building credibility, authority status, building trust, and then you can leverage that later on in other forms where you can. Initially it's not about writing the book but organising your thoughts about how you are going to help people, which I call at the academy the Unique Branded Solution. It's their framework because the framework comes before the book but that same framework then becomes the chapters and subheadings of a book and can also be the modules in an online program, also, it can be the segments of content for a workshop. When you initially create the framework, it becomes a less daunting task because you've already segmented the thoughts and ideas to go into the book.

Me: Is there any tip that you would like to share with the readers?

Andy: When writing, break it down into something that you can achieve, because most people don't, they just overwhelm themselves to the task because they see it as there's just too many things to do, so just start with one and get a little tick in the box.

Me: Awesome. I am aware how busy you are Andy so many thanks for your time and contribution in informing my readers how you used your book as a marketing tool for your business.

Andy: Thanks for having me. All the best.

As a speaker, I have learnt a lot from Andy Harrington and one thing which stands out is the authority and success that he has in his field. I am sure that all of the steps that he takes within his business are not taken lightly. There was definitely a thought process applied around the decision to write a book, so as they say 'the only way to be successful is to do what successful people do.'

Many thanks to Andy Harrington for sharing his experience and I am sure there are a few ideas that you can grab from that interview to use for your book.

The next chapter will be the bonus chapter written by a dear friend of mine called Martin Sharp. He will be addressing another area that I have come to realise is an effective tool to get your content out to the world. In a previous chapter I mentioned that you have to grow in your market, and the more people you can get your content out to the better, I had a wake-up call when I spoke at an event and a lady came to ask about one of my books. She wanted to purchase it but was not a reader, more of an audio person, so when she said "when your book is in an audio format please let me know," I had a real eye-opening moment. Martin is going to be talking you about exactly that. He'll be taking you through the exciting process of how to turn your book into an audible version.

How to Turn Your Book Into an Audible Version

By Martin Sharp

Would you like to have greater market reach for your book? And not only greater market reach, but also have more influence over your reader?

Now you've probably spent time pulling your book together, had it edited and formatted, published and marketed and are disappointed at the lack lustre royalties that are coming in. Picture this. You have double the royalties coming in each month as a passive income, further capitalising on your knowledge and leveraging your work. What if you had major corporations such as Amazon, Audible and Apple actively promoting your work to their customers who they already know will be interested in what you do? Imagine you are not only sharing your expertise and building your authority, you are also building a connection with the listener through the power of your voice. So, if you are looking for all these advantages, you need to create an audiobook. If you are unsure what an audiobook is, (also referred to as a talking book), it is a recording of the text of book that can be listened to. The origins of recorded spoken audio date back to the 1930's with titles for the blind, although it wasn't until the 1980's when the medium really took off with courses, books and news being provided on cassette or vinyl records before moving to CD. Today, with the technological advancements, audiobooks are downloaded directly to phones, tablets, computers, and other electronic devices so they can be consumed quicker, easier and cheaper with lower distribution costs for digital media.

You may be wondering why you should create your own audiobook? It is my belief that non-fiction books are best read by the author, as opposed to fiction, which are better read by a voice actor. This is because the listener gets a better appreciation of where the author is coming from and feels more connected to the content and message being delivered. Also, as factual books typically don't require multiple voices, the role of a director is limited or not required, and as the author is the narrator, no auditions or castings are required. Let's face it, no one knows your book better than you, right? Because you know your material better, you can then add the inflection, tone and pace that you had in mind when writing it. And it is these experiential touches that allow the listener/reader to get to know you more, hopefully like and trust you more as the AUTHORity that you are. With all this in mind there has never been a better time to capitalise on creating your audiobook. Afterall, you already have all the material written, and this will provide another passive revenue stream with some platforms offering additional bonuses for attracting new subscribers. Now you might be wondering who I am to be giving you advice on Audible, as it is true that I don't work for them, I'm not affiliated to them and don't have a background in being an audio engineer or content producer. Yet if you had been with me on the evening of June 10th 2015, you would be sitting in a corporate conference suite in the centre of Richmond, London. It is typical tiered corporate meeting room style with yellowing wood doors and skirting, complemented by cream walls and a swirly carpet that is great to cover up the many coffee spillages portrayed by the stale odour in the room. The chairs and tables are setup in a classroom style facing a projector screen and lectern, ready for the 'business building classroom' also known as how to write a book.

The sound in the room is a dulled hubbub, synonymous with the start of many corporate networking events, where strangers are meeting, eyeing each other up and approaching with conversations about the weather, traffic, sport or other triviality. The spectacle always reminds me of the description of the fight or flight response given in many books. Almost like you can read on each person's face if they consider the other food, a threat or a mate.

As a small, wizened old man with white hair approaches the front of the room, a hushed quiet descends across the room and those still standing shuffle into their seats. "Do you want to be seen as an authority in your field?" he says with his American accent "And do you want to make more money, because you are the authority in your field? If you answered yes to these questions, then you need to write a book!" I've always fancied writing a book, it has been on my long-term goals for quite some time without a date set, so it didn't get done. It was in that moment that I committed to myself that this would be the year I get the book written, that it would launch in 2016. Have you ever had things in your life that you really wanted to achieve but kept putting them off? Maybe you felt you weren't ready, or it wasn't good enough? Or perhaps you felt that no one else would want to read your material or that surely everyone knows what you are writing about? Potentially you were worried about making a mistake, being judged or simply people saying you are wrong? Well, to cut a long story short, especially as I have covered a lot of similar content on the fun of book writing and publishing my first book "Digital Transformation: The Significant 7 Imperatives for Delivering Successful Change in Complex IT Projects" launched in 2016. To be very specific, we had a soft launch on Amazon on the 20th September 2016 followed by a hard launch at an event held in Amsterdam on 26th November 2016. Here's the thing. Many publishers won't provide you with any marketing, PR or other promotional assistance, they simply expect you to do it. And I'm sure, if you are like I was, you probably have never tried to promote your own book before, yet you are quite happy to give it a go!

It was around this time that I was introduced to James Dewane. Now James is an ex-electrician who owns his own fantastic business school teaching electricians and trades people how to create a profitable local business. He looks a bit like Dr Evil from the Austin Powers movies with an Irish accent. He specialises in sales, marketing and positioning and is one of the most generous people I know in sharing his experience. And the conversation that evening over a lime and soda turned to how my book is going.

"I'm struggling to achieve the sales of my book that I hoped for James, I really wanted to help more businesses to be able to transform into taking advantage of the new digital technologies available for improved productivity, reduced operational expenditure and increased profitability. Yet I feel like I'm hardly making a dent!"

"So, what have you tried so far Martin, perhaps there are some other options?"

"Well James, I've read a lot around the subject and reached out for help and advice from fellow authors. I even developed a marketing plan that covered a website, bonus portal, LinkedIn, Facebook and Twitter content and a couple of book signings, all of which have been executed."

"Sounds like a lot of effort so far, but tell me Martin, who specifically are you targeting the book at and how would most of them read it?"

Have you ever had one of those conversation that set the machinery whirring in your mind so loud that you couldn't hear or remember the rest of the discussion? I don't know whether the word "how" was supposed to be "when" or "where" but using the word "how "sent my mind racing. Given my book was aimed for a younger version of me, how do I consume books, and what would be my preference?

For me, I like to make the most of my time, and given that I travel extensively, I don't like carrying lot of paper with me, including books. As such, I use Kindle and Audible extensively, in fact I have a bit of a process. I'll listen to a book on Audible when in the car, out for a walk alone or travelling on tube, trains or planes. If I believe I need to further study the material, I'll buy on Kindle, and if I need to make extensive margin notes, I'll order a physical copy on Amazon. Chatting to a few other fellow consultants, I found that many did the same thing. So, I could see the benefits in a multimedia approach.

However, I don't know about you, but I'm no sound engineer or voice actor and I have never produced an audiobook, so this was a bit more challenging. First there was all the terminology to understand and I had lots of questions such as:

- How do I get an audiobook onto Audible?

- Do I need to hire a voice actor?

- If I do it myself, what microphones will I need?

- Do I need a soundproof room?

- What do I record it on?

- How do I edit it?

- Who checks it and what is their requirements?

I started by reaching out to friends, fellow authors and colleagues, none of whom had tried to get an audiobook published on Audible. So, time for plan 'B.' Research. I read books, blog posts, the Audible website. I downloaded software, purchased a microphone and other gear then on the 20th December 2017 I sat down to record the first words of my first audiobook.

Each fifteen minutes of the book was taking an hour to record, then another hour to edit and that was only if I wasn't interrupted, which I'm sure you can imagine was difficult in a family home with three children and three dogs. In fact, the best time I found was between 6:00 and 8:00 in the morning when there was no one around.

By the 2nd January the moment had arrived to upload them. I had recorded all the audio, including the opening and closing credits and the sample. They were all edited, formatted and exported as required by Audible. So as the progress bar slowly ticked by from 1% to 100% mirroring the progress of the file upload, I breathed a sigh of relief as the final notice appeared stating the book was waiting to be approved. Time for another well-earned cup of tea.

Ten days passed, and I received this email:

Hello,

The ACX Quality Assurance Team has reviewed your recently-completed audiobook, "*The Digital Transformation Book: The Significant 7 Imperatives for Delivering Successful Change in Complex IT Projects* ". We have found 3 issues that must be corrected before we are able to process your audiobook for retail sale.

Below, we have listed the requirements not met, the files affected, and our recommended solutions:

- **Issue:** 12 files have a low RMS and are too quiet: *Please see attached document for a graph of affected files.*
- **Issue:** Files contain high RMS variance: Example: *01 Foreward.mp3* (+20dB increase @ 00:46)
  - **Requirement:** files measuring between -23dB and -18dB RMS
  - **Solution:** Please raise the overall RMS level of each file to within our requirement. For example, if a file's RMS is -30dB RMS, it must be raised +8dB to be within our -18dB to -23dB RMS requirement range.
- **Issue:** The files from this title do not meet our noise floor requirement.
  - **Requirement:** a maximum -60dB noise floor
  - **Solution:** In post-production, you may use noise gating or reduction to help reduce the noise floor. Please be mindful that incorrect use of this kind of software can lead to poor sound audio.
- **Issue:** The files from this title need to be re-edited because there are noises at their beginning and end.
  - **Requirement:** files free of extraneous sounds
  - **Solution:** Please remove any extraneous sounds that are found in these files.

After you have corrected the issue(s) above, follow these steps to submit the project for review:

1. Log into your ACX account, navigate to the In Production tab, and select *Title* from your list of projects.
2. Select "Edit" next to the files listed above to delete, replace, and upload corrected .mp3 files.
3. Confirm the files appear in the order they are intended to be heard.
4. Click "I'm Done".

Please be aware that the ACX QA review is not an end to end review of your production and you should always do a full edit, QC, and mastering pass before submission. This is important because errors in the audiobook could garner negative reviews on Audible, Amazon, or iTunes which could result in fewer sales.

Regards,

The ACX Team

QA Engineer, ACX

Oh dear! Gating? RMS? Noise floor? What language is this? Feels like more research is required. Enough to say that two more failed attempts and what felt like an encyclopaedia of consumed audio engineering knowledge that could have happily sunk an ocean liner. This was not defeat, it was doing what I should have done in the first place and used an expert for the expert bits so I did exactly that and received a job well done.

Having the Audible book doubled my royalties immediately, more than paying for the sound engineer within the first month. Not only that but it meant that I was helping more people.

The Digital Transformation book has won awards and achieved best seller status in the highly competitive category of leadership alongside Dale Carnegie, Napoleon Hill and Steven Covey. And I have continued to produce more written, audio and video content in my pursuit of helping businesses large and small grow, taking advantage of the age of opportunity we are now in. This is not because I have an in-built skill or natural talent for this, but because I created a process that works. As hopefully my experience illustrates, there are a few things to think about when looking to create an acceptable audiobook and even more if you want to submit it to benefit from Audible.

So, let's walk through what you need and how you can take advantage of your creative efforts by creating your own Audible creation therefore benefiting from more royalties and exposure.

I've discovered that there are seven key things you need to focus on to create an audacious audiobook, and for this I've created the 'Authoritative Audible Audiobook Accelerator.'

Authoritative Audiobook Accelerator

When I work with my clients who are creating their amazing audible books, we go through these seven key focus areas. This is because what I've found is that they have a number of key questions at different stages in the development of the audiobook and I'm sure you would agree that if you have unanswered questions you can get distracted in trying to find the answer to them rather than concentrating on the task at hand. Also, the seven key focus areas match the key development stages that you will go through when creating a book. This way if you want to see the whole map of the journey you are taking, you can do. And likewise, if you only want to concentrate on the next leg, you can drill down.

Now the first point, If you don't investigate this, you may find yourself breaking the law and liable for hefty fines or worse. When you understand this element, you are at the start of your audiobook golden pathway, and this is about rights.

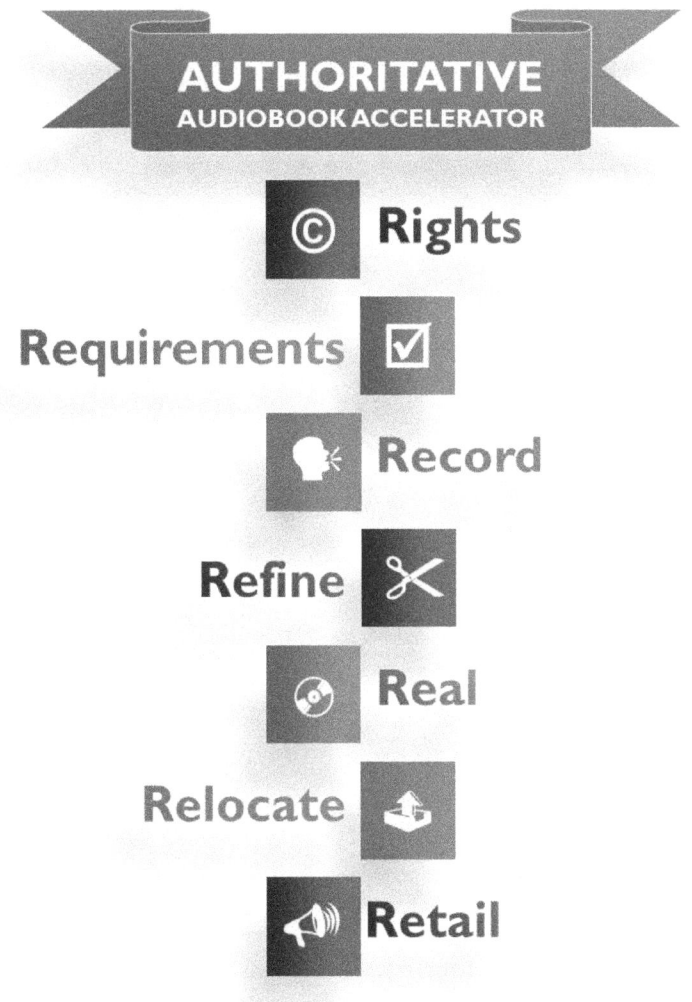

RIGHTS

So, what do I mean by rights? These are all the legalities regarding intellectual property ownership and copyright. Effectively, do you have the right to publish the audio version of your book?

If this is your first book and you haven't got a publisher or if you are self-publishing your book, then you are probably in a good position because you will not have signed any contract with a publisher or agent and therefore you are free to create your audiobook and reap the rewards in doing so. Because let's face it, in 2017, 2.2 million books were published according to UNESCO and Bowker reported that 1,009,188 books were self-published where only 79,000 (~3.4%) out of the 2.2 million were created as audiobooks. Would you agree that with a rise of 22% in listeners they deserve a broader range of books to enjoy where ever they are and, in a market where traditional paperback and eBook sales are declining with ever decreasing unit sale value, then your book deserves an audio edition?

For those who read the previous paragraph, are eager to get started but worried because you have a publisher and have concerns about the contract you've entered, then first of all, in the immortal words of Douglas Adams 'don't panic!' as the chances are that you will still be ok to create and publish your audiobook to the benefit of your readers and yourself.

You are probably wondering what to do about it at this point. Well first is to revisit the contract and read it through making any notes regarding audio rights or derivative works and such like. There are no standard contracts and each publishing house will have its own clauses, so there is no standard wording to look for. As with all contracts, if you are unsure then seek expert advice from a contract specialist and don't forget you can always speak to your publisher as they can give clarification.

REQUIREMENTS

Audible pride themselves on the quality of the audio publications they provide to their members and as one-off purchases. As you can imagine, to be able to publish a book on Audible, there are a number of requirements that you must meet, and as I outlined earlier, a Q and A process that you will need to pass.

Also, creating top quality audiobooks will help you maximize your sales potential by providing the best overall listening experience. So, would you agree that it would be best to have a good understanding of the requirements?

For this, you can find a full list on the ACX website:

https://www.acx.com/help/acx-audio-submission-requirements

What is ACX? ACX is a marketplace where authors, literary agents, publishers and other rights holders can connect with narrators, engineers, recording studios, and other producers capable of producing a finished audiobook, specifically published on Audible.

Why did I choose Audible? For me it came down to the numbers. When you look at other platforms, Audible has the greatest number of titles (with over 200,000 at the time of writing), and has the greatest number of listeners. Plus, using ACX, you can distribute you book via iTunes and Amazon at the same time. Audiobooks uploaded to ACX must adhere to these requirements. The ACX Quality Assurance team may reject titles that do not meet these standards, and your retail release may be delayed. Here is an example of some of the key requirements to help ensure listeners get a great experience.

Your submitted audiobook must:

- Be consistent in overall sound and formatting.
- Include opening and closing credits.
- Be comprised of all mono or all stereo files.
- Include a retail audio sample that is between one and five minutes long.
- Be narrated by a human.

Each uploaded audio file must:

- Contain only one chapter/section per file, with the section header read aloud.
- Have a running time no longer than 120 minutes.
- Have room tone at the beginning and end and be free of extraneous sounds.
- Measure between -23dB and -18dB RMS and have -3dB peak values and a maximum -60dB noise floor.
- Be at 192kbps or higher MP3 with a constant bit rate (CBR) at 44.1 kHz.
- Have 0.5 to 1 second of room tone at the beginning and end.

RECORD

Well done. You've made the decision that you want to release your works as audio into the world and you are probably eager to know what you need. You are probably wondering where to start and like many things, a little bit of preparation will go a long way.

With recording, this is especially the case. I've known people to use the microphone on their laptop or phone with devastating results, and likewise, others that have spent hundreds (and in some cases thousands) of pounds on professional equipment to again receive poor results. Yet with a little bit of planning and understanding you can achieve pro-quality audio on a modest budget. Like so many other things in life, if you start with good quality components and a simple yet effective method, you can create great results.

To help you with your shopping list and recipe method, here are seven items I've discovered that make a big difference to the quality of the product you produce to ensure that you put the investment into the right place.

SPACE

Let's start with where you will capture your voice. We don't all have the luxury of our very own recording studio with perfect soundproofed walls and sound engineer on hand gesturing to us through the glass panel of the isolation booth, (that booth where you sit and read your works to a professional condenser microphone). Yet the room that you record in will have a massive impact on your finished recording. By starting with a fantastic recording environment and taking the right steps during the mastering of your audiobook, you'll always produce audio ready to go to all the major audiobook vendors out there, while also providing a great listening experience. Ok, what things affect the room and why are they important to consider?

NOISE FLOOR

First, let's look at what sound engineers call 'noise floor.' Noise floor is the background sound inside the room you are recording in and sometimes is referred to as 'room tone.' This value occurs even in soundproofed isolation booths. When the door is shut and the outside world goes quiet, there is still sound in the booth, which could be your heart beat, your breathing or the hum of your computer.

I've heard some people ask, "why is it so important to eliminate all the sounds? I have phone calls, webinar and conference calls with noises in the room and no one complains?", which is a great question. The thing is, when you are on a webinar, conference call or telephone you are expecting the interruptions. You excuse poor quality sounds because you are interacting, and you usually only listen for a short burst of time. Have you ever noticed, especially with a webinar or online video, how you can usually piece things together if the video quality is poor or choppy, but struggle when the sound is poor or choppy? In fact, you are probably more likely to exit the call, meeting or stop watching the video if the sound gets too poor.

Listening to an audiobook can be quite a personal experience, especially if the listener is using headphones. You are literally in their ear, they have blocked out the rest of the world just to listen to you, which means with that amount of attention they will hear every single noise. Would you prefer that they listen to the words you are saying, start to ponder the meaning and work out how to integrate the teaching into their lives, rather than wondering whether the rattling noise in the background is a train or your central heating?

Now when working with a sound engineer, they will be able to notice every clink, clank, pop or crash. So, look around at the space where you are planning on recording. Do you have central heating or air-conditioning? If they create noise, can you switch them off? What about other electrical devices such as the high-pitched whine of a TV or set top box on standby for example. Can you unplug them? Is that the washing machine you can hear clanking and whirring, or the fridge or freezer compressor? What about the noise of the traffic outside, planes flying overhead, or the cooing of the wood pigeon in the tree outside the window. What about finding a time when these are the quietest?

Ask me how I know about all these. Well my first few recordings were dreadful, littered with all these erroneous noises, many couldn't be removed and required me to re-record chapters. How hard can that be you are probably thinking, and then there were the interruptions.

Chapter one: VVvvvrooooom of the vacuum cleaner. Hmmmm.

Start again. Chapter one. "Dad, where is my PE kit?" You have got to be kidding me, they know I'm recording!

Let's try once more. Chapter one. *Woof woof, woof woof.* Argh!!!! "Jack! It's only a cat passing by the French windows!"

At the start, every time I hit the record button, within seconds something would stop me from progressing.

Hopefully you can see how creating the quiet space physically and within your schedule so you won't be interrupted, is so important. That being said, you will be spending quite some time in your home studio space, depending on how long your book is and how many chapters you are going to read in one sitting. Therefore, you need to make sure you have a comfortable seating position and that you can see your work without having to move too much.

Let me present the next erroneous sound producing culprit, and let me say that there is nothing worse than a squeaky office chair, no matter how comfortable and executive it is, ruining a perfectly good recording session, and these are just to name a few of the many noise creating items.

One option is to purchase and use a dedicated audio recording device. These tend to be solid state (with no moving parts) and extremely quiet. Alternatively, if you have a quiet laptop with an SSD (solid state disk) then check to see if there is a low power option and close all applications other than the recording app to try and prevent the fans from whirring. If the laptop starts to warm up and the fans start whirring, shut it down and take a coffee break leaving it to cool before restarting. If you have a desktop computer or a laptop with a traditional hard drive with moving parts, the clicking and whirring is probably too noisy. So perhaps you could use the microphone, monitor, keyboard and mouse on extension cables, and keep the noisy computer out of the room.

NOISE DAMPENING

We've talked about the background noise in the room so now let's examine another technique which is 'noise dampening.' You may be wondering why we need to consider dampening the sound? Now remember back in those school science classes where they lectured about sounds being reflected off surfaces and that this is how echoes are created? You can see something similar if you fill a bowl with water and drip your finger into the surface and watch the ripples. Do you see how they bounce of the sides and how quickly it looks chaotic rather than like nice clear waves? It turns out that when recording these reverberations and reflections, no matter how small, they are picked up by your microphone and detract from a great sounding product. You have the same noise and chaos in the background. This is where the dampening comes in. You need to minimise the number of reflective surfaces in your space by utilising sound absorbing materials. If you are thinking about that isolation booth in our professional studio again, then you are right that they are covered on the inside with material such as egg crate foam or other material, which soften the sound by removing the reflections.

Now I'm not suggesting that you need to run out and cover the room you will use in grey egg crate foam tiles, as if it is a home studio and a temporary space you will be using. It will be a lot of expense and may not fit in with your décor. However, there are some practical things you can do to achieve a good result, simple things such as shutting the curtains in the room to prevent reverb off of the window (also helps deaden some of the sound). Hang covers over doors, tables and other hard surfaces. In my home studio bedroom, this had a great effect, didn't look great and I certainly had weird looks from my wife, but it is a second temporary use rather than being permanent studio, so I was fine with it.

Also think about the floor. If you are in a tiled room or one with a wooden floor, you will find that this will cause a significant echo and as such, a carpeted room would be best or look to place rugs and other floor coverings down to absorb some of the noise. If you are still hearing a bit of noise or looking to create cleaner, focused and more intelligible recordings, than you may want to invest in an isolation shield. These contraptions can stand on a desk or microphone stand with your microphone held in the centre, a bit like a series of small room dividers with great sound absorbing qualities.

STUFF

We have arrived at the part where if you purchase the wrong things you will epitomise the saying "all the gear and no idea", yet when you get this right, you can create a professional quality finish on what can be a modest budget. What we will be going through is some of the equipment that you will need inside your home audiobook studio.

Along with some 'do's and don'ts,' we will go through setups involving three different budget options aimed at whether this is your first book and don't want to spend a fortune, or you are already on with the idea of producing several books or video media products and beyond. This way you can see what sort of setup might work well depending on where you are on your audiobook journey.

With each piece of equipment, you need to know what you need, why you need it, and for those who need to know everything a bit of background information on each.

Let's get something on the table now. Having good equipment will make a difference, but just like creating the best space you can, you must not forget about the craft of performing. Giving a good experience and a good performance is what a lot of listeners are coming for, right? More on this later.

So, what should you be considering?

SOUND DEADENING

We've gone through why you need sound deadening, so what are some of your options?

- Egg crate foam tiles – This is quite a permanent solution. If you are looking to create a permanent space this is something to consider, however, if you are considering this option then you would be better to hire a sound expert to help you setup your studio professionally.

- Isolation booth – Yes, you can buy an isolation booth starting with one that is on stands and envelops the top half of your body, to those 1.2m x 1.2m, (if you paint it blue, you can pretend to be Dr Who at the weekend), through to sizes that would fit a whole band in. Be prepared to part with lots of money though and space.

- Sound deadening sheeting and matting – Is commonly used in vehicles and can be used as a temporary covering over hard surfaces or hung on walls.

- Blankets – You probably already have these under the bed, in the airing cupboard or elsewhere, so you benefit twice from their cosy warmth and from sound absorbing, non-reflective properties. This is the option I use.

- Isolation shield – These portable folding devices are covered with dense foam to prevent sound reflecting from the back or sides of the microphone. I personally don't like these as they don't prevent reflected sound from the front of the microphone or behind you, and you have nowhere to hold your book to read from.

AUDIO RECORDER

For your audio recorder you want to record the raw uncompressed audio, such as to a WAV file. This is because if you record to MP3 or MP4 or other compressed audio format, it makes the file smaller by taking bits of the file, your sound output and making approximations of it, reducing the audio quality. Then when you come to edit and master your file, you'll be making your own cuts and compressing it further reducing the audio quality. It's a bit like a strawberry flavour chewy sweet kind of tastes a bit like a real strawberry, but you can taste the difference when you eat a real strawberry, and you wouldn't want to start editing a strawberry flavour chewy sweet and expect to make an excellent tasting jam would you?

- Dedicated – Yes, you can buy a dedicated audio recorder. They look and work like a Dictaphone, however, you can connect external microphones to them for better quality sound.

- Laptop – These are great to use, and you'll find that your digital audio workstation will have the capability to record the sound for you. Just make sure that it has a solid-state disk (SSD) for storage, that you close all other applications and set to low power mode to reduce the risks of the fans cutting in because it is heating up.

- Mobile or tablet – These are good because they are silent, however you may have to compromise on the quality of the audio interface, which could introduce unwanted noise into your recording.

- Computer – Whether you are using a PC or a MAC, there is nothing getting away from the fact that computers are usually noisy beasts. Clicking hard drives, whirring fans, beeping, beepy things. If you do want to use your computer it would be best to invest in some extension cables for the monitor, keyboard, mouse and audio interface so that you can leave it outside of your recording space.

STORAGE

Where you are going to store your hard work, all those lovely words, all that lovely sound and lovingly captured as a digital audio file? These include:

- Locally on the device.
- Memory card.
- External storage device – beware that many of these will use spinning disks, which will make a humming noise.

Then get used to saving your file regularly just in case the application crashes. Let's face it, you have probably used Microsoft Word or other application in the past when it crashed and lost all your work because you didn't save regularly. In the past I have had clients call me at 3am when this has happened just before having to submit their works, and there is nothing you can do about it, even crying down the phone won't bring the unsaved content back from the digital ethereal plane. While dedicated audio recorders are less likely to crash mid-take, I would still advise periodically stopping and starting a new file. I'll let you choose what period, as that will be the maximum amount of loss you'll incur should something go wrong.

Now regardless of the media used, there are three important things to remember about your storage, these are:

- Backup
- BACKUP
- BACKUP!!!!

Technically I guess you could say that they are the same thing, but it is such an important thing I believe it is worth mentioning three times. You won't guess how many times I've had to help people try to recover their content due to a failure, corruption or simple mistake. While the relief on their faces and gratitude in their hearts is visible when it works, there is an equal number for whom the information is irrecoverable, and they may have lost years of work, some of it irreplaceable archive content or sound bites. The sad, solemn, grey look as the sheer horror of what has happened sinks in, is the look of someone who is grieving or has lost hope.

Yet, would you agree with me that there is a plethora of ways that this situation could have been prevented if only a little proactive action had been applied? Let's examine some of those.

- File copy – Yes, this is as simple as it sounds. Make a copy of your files onto another storage device such as an external hard drive, USB stick, memory card or other. This will mean if your computer or main storage device fails, or you delete your files, you can copy them back across. It also covers you if your copied storage device fails, because they are not immune from error. You can replace it and take another copy from the primary storage device.

- Cloud storage synchronisation – If you use a service like Dropbox, Microsoft OneDrive or Google Drive, you normally install an application (certainly on Windows or OSX) that will automatically synchronise files stored locally in their folder, up into the cloud when connected to the internet. Also, they usually retain a few versions or copies taken at different times should your file become corrupt or you need to work on an earlier copy. This is the option I use, as it takes away any manual copying on my behalf, reducing my admin and giving me peace of mind.

- Backup software or service – Another alternative is to use backup software or a service which will periodically take a copy to another disk or tape or into the cloud. This takes a bit more configuration but may be worth it if you use it in addition to one of the two above methods and you have a significant investment in your content.

So, become obsessive about saving your work and backing up your work or become depressed with rework and content loss.

AUDIO INTERFACE

This is how you are going to connect your microphone to your audio recorder. Like with many technology items, there are several different ways you could do this, each with their own benefits and drawbacks. For this section I am going to draw your attention to two aspects only. The first of these helps further reduce noise, because if you don't consider this, you could have the quietest space in the house and still pick up electrical hum. And this is using balanced vs unbalanced connection. But what do I mean by a balanced connection? This affects the buzzing noise you sometimes hear when on the phone or listening to music through speakers, even when the volume is at its lowest, and it is caused by all the other electrical devices around you. It's a bit like how an FM radio works. You cannot see the signals, but an aerial, a piece of wire or metal is needed so that all the radio waves can be collected and turned into sound by the radio receiver. The same thing happens with electricity. It is supplied in waves, usually between 50Hz and 60Hz depending which country you are in. These waves are then collected by your microphone cable and you hear this background buzz on your recording when using an unbalanced connection. Whereas, using a balanced connection helps reduce or remove this buzz by sending two lots of sounds from your microphone to the audio recorder that allows it to remove the electrical buzz that it may collect along the way.

The other aspect is the component that converts your voice into a digital file information stream that a computer is capable of storing and working with. This is the analogue to digital (A/D) converter. An A/D converter takes periodic samples, usually a minimum of 44,000 within a second for good quality, and stores the electrical values at that point as a digital record that can be converted back into audio. Now this is important because the better the A/D converter the better the sound quality as not only is the number of samples collected, but so also are the variations and subtleties, a bit like the difference between a black and white camera and a colour one.

So, what are the options:

- Built in – We'll come back to this when we talk about microphones. Fair to say, you should not be considering this option as in most cases the built-in microphones have been specified to a budget and not to the quality of sound.

- 3.5mm headset jack (microphone headphones as come with most phones) – these areas have 'unbalanced' inputs. This mean that they can pick up noise along the cable. If you are looking to record onto your phone, this could be an option, however the quality of microphones available for this interface are not usually adequate.

- 3.5mm microphone jack – some of these are "balanced", so worth checking with your device specification.

- XLR cable – This is a professional quality connection using three pins and will be 'balanced'. For use with a computer you will need an XLR to USB converter or pre-amplifier, which in many cases will come with a better-quality A/D converter built in. *This is the option I use.*

- It's worth noting that you can also obtain an XLR to 3.5mm headset or microphone converter or pre-amplifier. This could reduce some of the buzz by having a shorter unbalanced cable but will not provide a better A/D converter.

- USB – These have a microphone connected directly with the USB port on your computer (or Android or iPhone) and contains its own A/D converter. Good quality versions of these can provide a professional sound. However, beware as cheaper ones can be worse that simply using your headset from your phone! *This was the option I used on my first audiobook.*

MICROPHONE

We touched on not using the built-in microphone that is contained in your laptop or smart phone and now it is time to elaborate on why. As mentioned, in most cases, the built-in microphones have been specified to a budget and not to the quality of sound, so this is a compromise by the manufacturer. Also, the location of the microphone is not fantastic, usually surround by materials that will affect the sound and is subject to significant interference simply by being mounted on the same circuit board as all the rest of your device's components.

I've heard some people say, "it works ok for Skype calls, webinars and conference calls, why won't it work for audiobooks?" It all comes down to the quality of audio and the intimacy that is generated when listening. During a call you expect that there will be interference, other noise, the occasions call drop, etc. But with professional quality recordings like audiobooks or studio recorded music, everyone's standards increase and what they are willing to accept decreases. Can you imagine sitting down and relaxing to your favourite piece of music with all the interference, dropouts and interruptions you have on a conference call? You may not find it that relaxing. You are probably wondering then what microphone to use? Preferably you'll use a large-diaphragm condenser microphone, which tends to be the standard for professional audiobook recording with a separate XLR to USB pre-amplifier audio interface, but there are cheaper alternatives like this USB powered snowball microphones that offer similar performance for a lower cost. You are mainly trading off flexibility and control.

- Condenser – Condenser microphones have a thin conductive diaphragm that sits close to a metal back plate. As the sound pressure or vibration is captured from an active component phantom, power or batteries are usually required. These are ideal microphones for precision recording in a studio. *This is the option I use.*

- Dynamic – Dynamic microphones are very versatile and work by moving a magnet or coil to capture the sound. They are great in a variety of locations, but they can also change the character of the voice depending on the quality of the microphone.

- Shotgun – Shotgun microphones are not usually used in recording studios as they are designed to capture sound at a distance, such as when news reporting or shooting wildlife documentaries. This is due to the long tube design which channels the sound.

- Lavalier – Mainly used in presentations, the Lavalier microphone clips onto the clothing and if used well, can create a good quality sound. However, they suffer from picking up noise such as clothes rustling and are easily knocked or work loose when attached to clothing. If you are pushed on cost, the headset that comes with your iPhone or Samsung or other phone can double as a Lavalier microphone if you put the earpieces inside the buttons on your shirt and are great for impromptu recording when out and about.

- Headset – Headsets tend to be designed for conference calls, webinars and others, so will have a reduced frequency range, which will make you sound more mechanical. *This was the option I used on my first audiobook.*

One last point to note when choosing a microphone is, you will note that the manufacturers mention patterns. This is the area around the microphone that is sensitive to picking up sound. For recording in your studio, it is best to get one with a Cardioid pattern as it is designed to pick up sound only from the front of the microphone and reduces the erroneous sounds coming in from other directions.

SHOCK MOUNT

Just like Lavalier microphones can pick up sound from clothing, other microphones can pick up vibrations travelling into the microphone through the stand. These vibrations generate sound and we don't want that. What you can use is a microphone shock mount vibration remover, which mounts on your microphone stand and holds your microphone in a shock absorbing cradle preventing the vibrations from reaching the microphone.

POP FILTER

If you are wondering what a pop filter is used for, then you are asking the same questions I did when I started, which took me on a journey to learn about sibilance and plosives. If you've never come across sibilance and plosives, these are sounds made when pronouncing certain letters like P's, F's, T's, H's, S's and W's. These are usually harder sounds and can result in an increase in volume and distortion in your recording. To show you what I mean, hold your hand within 2cm from your mouth, then speaking naturally, say the alphabet. Pay attention to the air as it hits your hand, especially on the letters P, F, T, H, S and W. Now the microphone is acting like your hand except it converts the air pressure into electrical signals. So, a pop filter is a wind screen that is mounted 7cm or 3" from the microphone. Then you narrate another 7cm or 3" from the pop filter, so that the sound of your voice passes through the screening material, which deflects and minimizes sounds that can distort the recording like P's, F's, Ts, Hs, Ss and W's.

MICROPHONE STAND

Just as the name implies, this is what will hold your microphone and stand it up in the right position. So, you have decided where you are going to work, will you be standing or seated?

Some people say that you get a better sound when you are standing because your chest is fully open, and you are less likely to slump or slouch. I agree with this after experimenting, but it may not be an option for you. So, if you are sitting, try to make sure you are in an upright position and not laid back.

One of the most important things with a microphone stand is to make sure you have one that allows you to position your microphone at a comfortable level in line with and within 15cm or 6" of your mouth. Therefore, look for one that allows you freedom of adjustment. If you have a Lavalier or headset microphone, then this section is not applicable. Also, many USB microphones come with built-in stands and are not compatible with microphone stands, so with these you will have no choice other than perhaps using books or other items to adjust the height and make it more comfortable.

Stands tend to come in 4 styles:

- Desktop – As the name implies, this stand usually sits on your desk and usually has adjustment for height. They will take up space and may be awkward to work around.

- Mounted arm – Like a desktop stand, they are designed for working at your desk but don't take up space on the desk itself. Instead they are usually mounted onto the side of a desk with a clip or clamp and have either a mechanical arm or gooseneck that allows the microphone to be positioned in the right space. Many films and TV programmes that show radio studios will have the microphone mounted on one of these. *This is the option I use.*

- Free standing straight – Fancy yourself as a lead singer or possibly you want to imagine what it is like to be Mick Jagger? Then this is the typical robust microphone stand. Very solid and stable with height adjustment.

- Free standing boom – Like the straight stand but has an adjustable boom which can be adjusted to allow the microphone to be positioned over the top of something such as a piano, your script stand or your desk. *This is the option I also use.*

CHAIR

If you have decided to use a chair, then as mentioned previously, make sure you select a silent one. The squeaks and groans from old wooden chairs, executive office chairs or rocking chairs are going to spoil what will be a great recording session. Ensure you are sitting comfortably before you begin, with enough support and preferably in an upright posture to allow for the best possible sound from your voice.

TABLET

In yesteryears you would have had to worry about the rustling of the papers of your book or manuscript when narrating. However, today we have a great advantage in that we can read our works from a tablet, moving through the pages with a silent movement of your finger over the screen. Android, Windows and Apple based tablets allow you to use Microsoft Word, Google Docs or Adobe reader, with the first two having a reading mode, which will make it easier for you to adjust the size of the text for reading and removing unnecessary items like page headers and footers.

SCRIPT STAND

As you will be reading your works, it is best to have it positioned where it is easiest for you to read. If you're using your own desk you may find that this is normal and comfortable for general working but may cause your chin to rest on your chest. This will alter the quality of your voice, so you may want to increase the height so that it is more in line with your eye level or just below it.

If you are standing then you could hold your tablet, although on extensive sessions you may find your arms aching, so I would recommend picking up a music stand that can be adjusted to a comfortable reading height.

LIGHTING

You won't want to get eye strain or feel tired during your sessions so make sure that you use lighting that is easy on the eyes. Avoid fluorescents or lighting that is too bright or dim. Also avoid anything with a dimmer as these cause flickering and electrical noise that can be picked up by your microphone.

VOICE

Your voice can wear out, especially if you are talking a lot, which is kind of a side effect of narrating your book. Therefore, it is important to look after it. Here is a collection of advice that I received when I first started and use when recording and continue to do today:

- Sleep – Make sure you are well rested as the quality of your sleep will affect the quality of your voice. I won't go into the rejuvenating effects of sleep as there are lots of books and studies that you can read around this. Just take it from me that it works!

- Avoid smoking and alcoholic drinks the night before and during the sessions.

- Don't talk – Where possible try not to talk and certainly not shouting or yelling the night before your recording sessions.

- Drink room temperature or warm drinks - Room-temperature water soothes the vocal cords and opens the oesophagus. Ginger tea is particularly beneficial for the throat. Drink as much tea as you like to keep your throat relaxed and ready. Adding honey provides a bit of a coating for your throat. Drink plenty of water prior to and throughout your recording session. Don't drink ice water, as it can tighten the vocal cords. Refrain from drinking coffee the day of your recording session. The acidic properties in coffee are dehydrating and may have a negative effect on the throat. Also avoid caffeinated drinks as they are a diuretic and you'll find yourself spending a lot more time running to the toilet.

- Avoid fizzy drinks especially on the day of recording as they will make you feel bloated and can give you gas, another session-spoiling sound.

- Avoid foods that give you mucus – Some people have a reaction to dairy or gluten products that produce excess mucus in their nose and throat, which will affect the quality of your voice.

DIGITAL AUDIO WORKSTATION

Digital Audio Workstation or DAW is the software that you will use to edit and master your work and you could also use it for recording your work. This is specialist software, which is a bit like Microsoft Word but whereas Microsoft Word allows you to write your work using a keyboard, then afterward spell check it for errors, correct grammar, adjust the formatting or copy and paste sections around, and print and publish it. Your Digital Audio Workstation will allow you to do similar for audio files. You can capture your audio (write it), check it for noise, errors or other quality problems (spelling and grammar). Delete or move sections within the file and apply filters and effects (formatting) and encode it (print it).

There are a variety manufacturers and vendors of DAWs such as Audacity, Adobe Audition CC, Logic Pro X, Pro Tools, Reaper Studio, FL Studio, Ableton Live, Twisted Wave and WaveLab. Each with many different options ranging from free to very, very expensive and some DAWs are better for editing while some are better for recording, better for mastering and some have other options like destructive versus non-destructive editing, as in whether your original files are modified during editing – destructive or if the changes are stored elsewhere such as on a duplicate so you can always go back to the original – non-destructive.

Going through each of these is a chapter (and beyond) in its own right. For ease and as an introduction to DAWs we will look at Audacity. Audacity is a free and open-source DAW that you can download for Windows, Mac or Linux from their website https://www.audacityteam.org/

It is good for editing and you can record fine. The only couple of areas that let it down is that it performs destructive edits, meaning that changes are made to the original files. Therefore, it is worthwhile taking a copy before you start, just in case you need to come back to the originals. The other is that you cannot apply filters, effects or plugins "on the fly" while listening to the audio. So, you make the changes, then listen to them, which can take a while to process if you have chapters at the maximum 120 minutes as specified by Audible. If you don't like the changes, you have to undo them, wait for the computer to process the audio, then try another set. This can be time consuming and may result in introducing other audio anomalies if you get frustrated and try to rush.

Another popular commercial tool is Pro Tools, which at the time of writing has a 16-track free version available called Pro Tools First. The chargeable version scales to 256 tracks for recording professional music, so each instrument has its own track. As a narrator you probably will only need 2 or 3 tracks depending on whether you want transition music between chapters or not. You can download this from https://www.avid.com/pro-tools-first

Pro Tools allows you to perform the post-production processing (filters, effect or plugins) "on the fly" while listening to the audio and apply the changes to your audio file in a non-destructive way, so your original is not lost. Some people say for audio narration, Pro Tools is the workhorse of the DAW market, an industry standard for some.

PLUGINS AND FILTERS

We touched on filters and plugins when going through the DAW, but you may be asking yourself what are filters and what are they used for? Whether you are just starting out, or you're a seasoned pro, you often need to fix common audio problems and that is where you need plugins and filters, your tool bag of audio repair technology. With a few clicks you can modify your audio after you've captured it. Now, I'm not talking about being able to isolate a singular noise out or enhance a muffled sound like an FBI forensic sound engineer would do as portrayed in films and on TV. What we are looking at is how to deal with some of the more common problems that may creep into your audio even though you have setup your room. These include:

- Noise remover.
- Equalizer.
- Reverb remover.
- De-esser and plosive remover.
- Voice leveller.
- De-clipper.

- Compressor.
- Final gain.

These plugins and filters are usually provided as Virtual Audio Technology (VST) files and work with a number of DAWs including Audacity and Pro Tools.

To explore a selection of filters and audio processing plugins, you can have a look at:

- Accusonus ERA Bundle 3 https://accusonus.com/products/audio-repair/era-bundle-standard
- Reaper ReaPlugs VST FX suite https://www.reaper.fm/reaplugs/

You can also find plugins that will help you in mastering your final version before submitting to the Audible QA process.

- Audacity ACX Check Plugin https://wiki.audacityteam.org/wiki/Nyquist_Analyze_Plug-ins

HEADPHONES

Ok, you may be thinking that "I already have headphones, I don't need to worry about this" or "what do I need headphones for, I'm narrating not listening!"

And the thing is, there are different types of headphones that are useful in different situations.

For example, you may want to monitor how you sound as you are speaking, so that you can pick up possible issues in your studio like other noises seeping in. For this you would want to have closed back headphones, meaning the back of the headphones don't have any grills or spaces that will allow sound to escape or other sounds to leak in. While if you are wanting to hear exactly how the recording sounds, you probably want to use open-backed headphones that don't cover the back of the headphones and allow freer movement of the air as the sound pressure is able to move out of the headphones, resulting in a better quality sound where you can pick up more of what has been recorded. However, these do leak noise that could be picked up by your microphone and let background noise in. These can be either over the ear or in the ear version.

Other than the microphone picking up the noise, this is less of a concern when narrating than it is if you are recording music, but if you do want to monitor yourself while narrating, I recommend getting closed back headphones.

For me it is more important to have headphones for editing and I use two different types to understand how different it may sound for the listener, because for me that experience is what is important:

1. Over the ear Sennheiser open backed
2. In the ear Bose QuietComfort closed backed

SETUP

Ok we have the gear and are looking to start recording. We open the Digital Audio Workstation, Audacity and need to make some adjustments to the settings. These are needed for a couple of reasons. First is to ensure that the Audible ACX QA requirements are met and the second is to create an organised working folder structure for you to save your work into.

Let's start by setting the recording device to the correct microphone. This is a common mistake! Many people plug in their really expensive microphone into their computer's USB port and don't realize that Audacity is still set to the default choice which is usually the tiny-tinny microphone built into the computer. If you've plugged a microphone into your USB port, the correct setting is probably 'Microphone (USB Audio Device).' If you are using a pre-amplifier with a professional microphone, it will probably be the name of the interface manufacturer such as 'Focusrite USB (Focusrite USB Audio).'

Next, set your recording channel to 'mono recording channel' as you only have one source of sound, that being your voice as most microphones are monophonic. Also, this will prevent phasing or harmonic problems later on and as you probably are not sampling a racing car or something going from left to right, the balanced audio of your voice in both ears will be more pleasant to the listener. Some people think that because the majority of people listen to stereo music through stereo headphones, mono recordings will only come out of one side left or right. This is not true, you have the capability to PAN the placement of the sound between the left and right. Next, set the project rate (Hz) to 44100, sometimes represented as 44.1kHz. This is the recording rate or sampling frequency and means that the electrical value of your microphone will be sampled 44,100 times per second with the value being saved to the audio file. Why 44.1kHz you may be thinking? Well this is the same as CD audio sound quality as defined by Sony. This was based on the human hearing range being roughly between 20Hz and 20,000Hz and the Nyquist Shannon sampling theorem that states that any sampling frequency must be greater than twice the maximum frequency it needs to reproduce, so greater that 40kHz. To finish off this highly technical bit there is one other statement you may read or see, and this is the number of bits sampled, also known as the bit depth. This will need to be set to 16 bits per sample as a minimum, the same as CD quality sound. You could increase this to 21 or 24 bits per sample, sometimes known as professional audio, although for narration there is little value in increasing this and there is an overhead on the power of equipment needed to cope with this.

Finally set the meter/wave-form dB range set to -96 dB (PCM range of 16-bit sampler) extend the monitor window or plot spectrum window, (those green/amber/red bars that bounce across the screen on your DAW as you speak). This way you can see how silent your room is and ensures that your voice is within the range required by Audible/ACX.

For your recording you want the raw audio to be captured without any filters or effects. This is because you want to be able to control how these are applied, some to the whole audio, others like plosive removal to small areas.

Let's now consider where you will store all your audio files.

First, have a master folder that will contain all your audiobook productions. For me, I have this as my Dropbox synchronisation location so that they are automatically backed up. Then create a folder for your audiobook in the master folder. Save each chapter as an Audacity project of your audiobook as a WAV, with the specs above, to this folder, naming each file with its section number first, then the section name.

RMS

What is RMS? In terms of Audible requirements and DAWs, RMS is an average measurement of sound pressure level, which you might think of being a bit like volume that was picked up by the microphone and stored in the recording as an audio file. The peak measures the loudest volume reached, and the noise floor measures the loudness of your room tone. You should only tweak these settings after you're done the editing/processing and the files are ready to be exported. RMS for each file must measure between -23dB and -18dB with peak values below -3dB, and a maximum -60dB floor.

START

While they may want to know the information you are conveying, they certainly don't want to be hearing a monotone drone. Not only is this boring but you are likely to put them into a trance where they won't retain anything. Remember people learn very little when asleep and a lot less when dead! Therefore, aim to make the very best recording you can the first time around. Be well prepared. Make sure you're rested, well-fed, comfortable and familiar with the material.

If you don't get a good initial recording, you'll have a very tough time producing a great product profitably. And there are a number of things to think about such as what to wear and eat, how to position yourself at the microphone and some of the basics of recording. To start with, you should be prepared! Know your book, get familiar with the structure and practice pronunciations. Now this may sound crazy given that you have written your book. However, it may be that you didn't write your book starting at page one and going logically through to the last page one at a time. You may have dived into different sections as the muse took you or perhaps you changed the structure during editing to make it easier to read or make more logical sense.

Don't use audio compressors, expanders, limiters or gates when recording. You want the raw sound as you record it from your microphone, then you can modify the sound using these plugins and filters in post-processing.

Make sure that you record 'room tone' at the start of every session. This is 15-30 seconds of 'air' that you'll use during editing if you need to create a space between sections. Leave your mobile phone, keys, jewellery or other noise generating items outside of your studio! Wear a silent wardrobe of soft cotton shirts and trousers, rather than a starched shirt, corduroy leggings and a Gore-Tex jacket. And remember, if you're using your computer to record your audio, turn off all alerts, notifications, unnecessary programs and applications to make sure you are not interrupted mid-flow.

SUCCESS

You'll find a lot of good books dedicated to the craft of audiobook performance. There are also many great schools and workshops you could attend to help you become an even better narrator. I encourage you to read and study a lot and practice a lot. As a business book narrator there are a number of things we don't necessarily need to do, such as handling characters, dialects and accents or other characterizations. We don't need to imitate strong narrators. This does not excuse monotone, monotonous and mundane narrations that will send your listener into a trance or potentially kill them off completely. Well, kill them off ever listening to you again, whether recorded or in person, which if you are creating the audiobook to help generate business, will obviously have the wrong intention.

So, what are the elements of great and successful narration?

- Training – Good use of your voice is essential to a great performance. So, training in public speaking, oration or acting will come in very helpful. Especially cover speed, timing, rhythm, tonality, inclination, inflections and how to convey meaning beyond the words spoken.

- Preparing well – Read the book. Add markings where you may want to emphasise a point, speed up or slow down. Convey concern or lead with a call to action. Jot down any words you aren't certain how to pronounce correctly and look them up.

- Working at the level of the paragraph – Trying to record a whole chapter in one sitting can be daunting, so aim to complete a number of paragraphs, save them and start on the next batch. This way you will stay fresher taking regular breaks and your voice won't wear as quickly. Plus, if you lose a file for any reason either technical or by your own mistake, you only need redo a small portion.

- Mark errors – You are going to make mistakes, admit it, accept it and move on. But when you are recording, so that you can find these quickly after, clap your hands loudly, wait a moment, then continue from the beginning of the sentence.

- Punch and Roll Record – This is an advanced method of creating a rough edit when recording, as it enables you to correct errors easily during the course of a recording session. You can stop, back up over a mistake, and continue recording, resulting in one track that eliminates the errors and is properly timed, without the use of cutting, pasting and clip-moving commands, or mixing of multiple tracks. You can perform these rough edits as you go, with minimal interruption of your performance and saving you time later when editing.

ROOM TONE

Room tone is the sound of your recording environment while you aren't narrating, which is especially noticeable at the beginning (head) and end (tail) of each chapter. Essentially you are recording the 'noise floor' that was mentioned earlier.

Now, remember back to those Audible ACX requirements where it states that each individual file must contain between 0.5–1 second of room tone at the head, and between 1–5 seconds of room tone at the tail. Why is this important? Well, as you've probably realised, even silence isn't silent in a studio. Even the best soundproof recording studios aren't silent, so when a listener is presented with a complete absence of sound, it is uncomfortable and jarring. So, the room tone is used as the reference to silence. A bit like 0°C is not absolute zero (zero Kelvin) that would be -273.15°C, but for everyday use, 0°C is cold enough.

CREDITS

Just as with a film, the credits are the people involved, the copyright information and details of the book itself. Audible ACX state that '*At minimum, the opening credits must note the name of the audiobook, the name of the author(s), and the name of the narrator(s). Closing credits must, at minimum, state "the end"*'.

However, there is nothing stopping you from adding further information into the opening and closing credits such as your website URL or landing page where they could find out more. Therefore, consider the following:

Opening Credits:

- Title of audiobook.
- Subtitle of audiobook.
- Written by (name of author.)

- Narrated by (name of narrator.)
- Bonus material available at (website or landing page URL.)

Closing Credits:
- This has been (title of audiobook.)
- Written by (name of author.)
- Narrated by (name of narrator.)
- Copyright (year and name of copyright holder.)
- Production copyright (year it was recorded) by (company name.)
- More information available at (website or landing page URL.)

SAMPLE

Thinking back to the Audible requirements, you will need a sample that you will give away to potential listeners to entice them into listening to the whole audiobook. As such, you should choose five minutes from your book that has dialogue and is exciting. I mean really exciting. This is like the first ten minutes of a movie where you have to make the decision whether you'll invest the time to watch the rest or not. I'm sure you've watched a great movie before that had you hooked in the first ten minutes and after that you just had to watch the rest?

It is that piece that you want to be giving away. Use the best bits in the five minute audio sample and either record this separately or create a copy of it when editing later.

SPECIAL

Whispersync for Voice will promote your Audible book to Kindle readers and your Kindle eBook to Audible listeners so they can enjoy an immersion reading experience Why is this important? Only 50,000 are Kindle eBooks with Audible Narration, which means if your listener or reader has one version they are more likely to be offered the alternative. If they have the audiobook and the eBook, they are more likely to remember your content and you. For this to work you must record audio word for word in an unabridged fashion, in English or German. There is a low tolerance for adlibs, improvised or misread content. The Audiobook needs to be 97% the same as the text in the eBook.

REFINE

In this section we are going to refine the raw audio, mistakes and everything, making it something that flows as an audiobook should. We are going to edit it.

It takes practice to become truly skilled at recording and editing but doing a great job at both will make a significant difference in your finished product. Here are some tips and techniques on how to edit the raw audio into chapters.

The key to successful editing comes down to three things:

- Listen first! Take a few minutes to sit back, close your eyes and really listen to the performance.
- Get familiar with keyboard shortcuts of your DAW.
- Listen again!

All DAWs have similar tools and you can think of them in a similar way to using your favourite word processor, like Microsoft Word, Google Docs or Apple Pages.

You can position your cursor along the timeline of your audio file to the point where you want to make a change. Then you can select the length you want to remove or cut or copy, then if you want to move it elsewhere, position the cursor along the timeline where you'd like to paste it and add it back in.

Here's the thing, remember you clapped each time you made a mistake? These claps appear as spikes in the audio timeline, so you can easily find where you need to make the first edits.

As with Microsoft Word, Ctrl+Z known as undo, is your best friend. If you've deleted, cut, copied, pasted or made other changes in your file that you want to reverse, pressing undo will revert you back to before that change.

QUALITY CONTROL AID

It you've decided to hire a professional audio engineer, or you want to listen through to spot problems before you start editing, then you may want to create a quick shorthand to capture the proposed edits on.

First, let's list as many of the common problems you would like to correct and give them a shorthand abbreviation for each type:

- Mr=misread – This will need you to narrate this part of the book again.

- Pron=pronunciation – This will need you to narrate this part of the book again.

- Dic=diction – This will need you to narrate this part of the book again.

- Nz=noise – This may be removable through editing or post processing. However, if very bad, it may need you to narrate this part of the book again.

- Pl=plosive/ sibilance - This may be removable through post processing. However, if very bad it may need you to narrate this part of the book again.

- Dist=distortion - This may be removable through post processing. However, if very bad it may need you to narrate this part of the book again.

You can then use a table like the one below to capture these, one row per problem.

Chapter/Section	Page	Line	Time	Type	Comments

REAL

Time to make it real or in audio terms, master your audio or the post processing. To many, this is the most mystifying part of audiobook production. Getting a good result requires a bit of trial and error, however, what you do in mastering can be undone and you can try again. Plus, if you're consistently recording in the same space using the same recording settings, you'll be able to save your mastering settings and use them repeatedly for every audiobook you produce.

Now, that edited file that we have refined and checked that the spoken words are what was written isn't the finished audio product. It is in this final mastering stage that allows you to improve the overall sound of the recording. If we remember from earlier in the chapter, all files submitted to ACX should measure between -23dB and -18dB RMS, with peaks hovering around -3dB. Your noise floor should fall between -60dB and -50dB. This along with all the other ACX requirements need to be brought together in this stage.

And that's it! Ok, so the devil is in the detail and something that again will take longer than a few paragraphs to really do it justice. But in the true provision of great value service fashion, lets quickly overview some of the more commonly used tools in the spoken word production and how they work to improve audio quality.

- Noise remover, equalizer (or EQ for short) – This is your first 'go to' tool when it comes down to getting rid of the low frequency rumble and high frequency airiness that marks a lot of amateur recordings.

- Reverb remover - Reverb is the unavoidable result of room acoustics. It can make your audio sound distant, 'echoey' or hollow. A reverb remover can reduce excessive reverb and bring your sound into focus, add clarity and clean up your dialogue.

- De-esser and plosive remover - Harsh sibilance and plosives (or p-pops) that haven't been reduced by a pop filter and an ideal microphone can be reduced or removed with this tool.

- Compressor – Acts like an automatic volume controller making the softer parts loud and louder parts softer, providing a steady, pleasant level to the listener.

- Voice leveller or final gain or normaliser - Gain inconsistencies are common in recordings. They often happen as a result of intentional or unintentional speaker movement, non-ideal microphone positioning or heavy audio editing.

My main takeaway is to play with the tools, to get used to what the different settings, effects and filters do so that you know in the future how to use them.

ENCODING

Encoding is the last step before you upload your audio files to ACX. In order for your audiobook to be released for sale, it needs to be encoded as, at a minimum, 192kbps CBR (constant bit rate) MP3s, with audio sampling at 44.1Khz, with each chapter in a single file and no file longer than 120 minutes. The entire audiobook must be either mono or stereo, not a combination. We recommend mono, as it reduces the chance of problems like phasing, accidental pans, etc. If a chapter or section is over 120 minutes long, then you will need to find a good break in your narration and split it into two files. If the section began with a header, such as 'chapter two,' start the second file with 'chapter two continued.' This will help listeners easily navigate between sections.

With your file open that you want to encode, select export or bounce and ensure the settings are correct with a good filename to help you identify each chapter or section.

Congratulations! Your audio files are now ready for submission.

RELOCATE

Now you've spent the time to record your book, edited it to remove the mistakes and mastered it so that it is ready to be published on Audible. The next step will make your audiobook available to listeners, where as missing this step will mean you are the only person who can enjoy your works, unless you try to distribute it yourself. This step is to upload your works to ACX.

If you haven't setup your ACX account, then do so now. Find your book using the search and click 'that's my book' and link it with the physical and eBook entries provided on Amazon and KDP.

Select 'I already have audio files for this book and I want to sell it.' Now upload the mastered copies, paying attention to keep them in order and having no spaces. Follow on-screen prompts and upload your mastered audio files.

Sit back and relax while you wait for ACX QA to complete.

TROUBLESHOOTING

So, you've completed your audiobook and are sitting back feeling rather happy with yourself at a job well done, when you receive that email from the ACX QA team and wonder, 'why did my title fail QA?'

All incoming audiobooks are put through a brief QA (quality assurance) check by the ACX Audio team. This check is done to ensure your audiobook is well produced, will meet Audible's customers' standards, and adheres to the ACX Rules for Audiobook production. Unfortunately, audiobooks do not always pass this QA check and it's the job of the ACX team to find the problems that require fixing before they can offer your title to the Audible listeners. Every minute you spend fixing these problems is a minute your title is not available for sale.

So, in order to help you avoid five of the most common problems that the ACX QA team come across, here is a brief list of what they are:

1. Improper grouping of files – Each file you upload should only represent one chapter or section.

2. Duplicate chapters and/or missing chapters – Make sure you upload the files in order and don't click done or approve if any of the files are missing.

3. Outtakes (aka bad editing) – This is where you may have stumbled over a word and left it in, rather than editing it out replacing it with the correctly pronounced word.

4. Extreme noise reduction – This is a sign of a poor recording environment and over-compensating using filters and plugins during post processing.

5. Gating – This is a process used to help reduce unwanted noise in a recording, which when used badly can negatively affect the quality of the sound and detracts from the listening experience.

Finally, remember that there is no substitute for having a great silent space created and good editing. If you are struggling, then it may be best to hire a sound engineer to help you with the mastering.

RETAIL

Now here I would normally run through your marketing, pre-launch, at launch and post-launch, however this was already covered earlier in the book regarding physical and eBooks. The same premise and processes apply. Its all about what you can do to get your audiobook noticed and drive people to it. There is one element though that is different and that is the cover art. Now like a book cover, many of the same rules apply; that it clearly shows the title, subtitle and author, displays who wrote the foreword and the location of any bonus material found on a website. The colours and imagery should be eye catching and appeal to your target listener.

So, as we have learned so far there are also some requirements from Audible that need to be considered, such as:

- Must contain both the name of the title and author(s).
- Cannot refer to physical media (such as CD's) other than the audio presented.
- Cannot show scans of jewel cases, promotional stickers, or cellophane.
- No pornographic or offensive materials.

If you are hiring a graphic designer or artist to create your book cover, then it would be good to let them know about the Audible requirements. That way they can tailor both covers to be similar, just different sizes. Which reminds me, you'll need to know the Audible cover art technical requirements. These are:

- JPG, PNG, or TIF file format only.
- No smaller than 2400 x 2400 pixels.
- No smaller than 72 dpi resolution.
- 24-bit (true colour) minimum.
- RGB colour (not CYMK).
- Images must be a true square, not a rectangular image with borders.
- File name should be the condensed book title using alphanumeric characters only.

Now sit back, reap the rewards of your hard work through increased royalty payments, greater distribution of your works backed by some of the biggest companies in the world, and share your knowledge and expertise with the people you are looking to serve and to help.

CONCLUSION

After having gone through all the information provided, there should be no reason for you not to take that next step in commencing your book journey if you haven't already done so. I want to conclude by speaking about one thing which I have noticed that has either prevented individuals from starting or completing the process and sometimes still ends up being an issue even after the book is finished and ready for publishing. The four-letter word which prevents many of us from taking the step with anything at all, and that is fear. For many, it's not that they don't have the information or aspirations to write a book, but they hold back mainly because of fear and self-doubt.

After having a conversation with a client of mine yesterday, who despite her book being complete and ready for publishing, did not given the go-ahead for the book to be published. This was due to her being scared of what people may say. I realised that it is a crucial element to mention.

Here's the thing. People will always talk whether you do good or bad but the question you have to ask is, what is more important, the few naysayers or the fact that you will be unleashing a masterpiece, something that will live on for a lifetime and transform lives?

Here are seven main points I believe you need to pay attention to if you want to prevent fear being the factor that keeps you from taking action.

1. Don't be perfect. Be prolific – perfectionism is a killer of dreams.

2. Stop thinking about what other people will think, instead, think about what you will think or feel about yourself if you don't do it, think about the sense of achievement that you will have.

Don't be perfect. Be prolific – perfectionism is a killer of dreams.

3. Do not allow the fear of criticism to set in; you will be criticised in life no matter how good you are or what you do.

4. Get rid of the fear of rejection by thinking more about the people your message will help rather than the ones that will object.

5. Stop thinking you are not good enough. You knew enough to get you to the point of where you are now and know enough to help someone else get there. You only need to be one step ahead; that makes you enough as they have not yet taken that step (Imposter Syndrome).

6. Ditch the fear of success. The focus is no longer about you, but more about your client and their journey

7. Fear of inadequacy is very similar to the fear of not feeling enough, however, here I am talking about the feeling that you do not deserve to be seen as an authority, expert or someone that others should appreciate, look up to or to even be called an author.

They are all lies that you should not be telling yourself. As I mentioned before, it's no longer about you. I had to overcome these fears and if I hadn't, I would not be able to assist and make an impact on the lives I already have and still will. I believe it is your time to shine, your time to make your voice and message be heard. Someone is waiting for your message; someone is waiting for you. Procrastination kills dreams, so don't be a murderer.

A story not told, is a message not heard and a life not saved.

Who Is Michelle Watson?

Michelle Watson is an entrepreneur, best-selling author, multi award winning speaker, certified personal development coach, speaker trainer, business coach and business book creation mentor & publisher. As founder of, **Breakfree Forever Publishing & Breakfree Forever Consultancy Ltd**, Michelle has done phenomenal work in growing her brand and dedicates herself to transforming the lives of many worldwide '*to go from being ordinary to extraordinary through the art of personal development, writing and speaking.*' Her numerous affiliations & recognition surround her passion for life transformation, motivation, vision creation and financial growth. Michelle's core passion is influencing individuals, families, entrepreneurs and organizations to achieve their personal, financial and entrepreneurial goals.

Michelle is a sought-after speaker and has worked with some very highly influential individuals to accelerate transformation and impact. Michelle has released 3 books including her bestseller *"Overcome & Rise Above – How to Turn the Downside of Your Challenges into The Upside of Renewing Your Life"* followed by *"Rise Above & Believe –It's Do or Lie – How to Get Rid of Excuses & Create the Life You Desire"* and also an E-book titled *"Women Be – 7 Tips to Create the Life You Desire."*

Michelle is known as an inspiration with her open honesty, bold, bubbly yet powerful personality, that shines with passion and has motivated thousands all over the world within the last 4 years and has won numerous awards reflecting her impact. Her uplifting character, warmth and humour, will leave you challenged and inspired to take the actions necessary to bring about change. Michelle will show you how to break-free, believe and build in order to create the life you not only desire but deserve. Michelle has empowered her audience through various media's such as SKY TV, The Digging Deep Show, Power Xtra Radio, Stand Out Woman Radio, Oasis Universal Radio, Harold Hill Radio, featured in Womelle magazine and numerous events across the globe.

Michelle firstly began with her dedication to giving back to her community via her Women Be event which enables women to break-free from their circumstances, believe in themselves & learn techniques on how to start a business & build a brand.

Michelle is an overcomer against all odds and teaches through her various seminars, masterclass and programmes how to overcome your current circumstances and create the life you desire.

Michelle is a Co-Pastor, wife, mother of three children and is the pure essence of success, born in London but raised from the age of 3 in the country of Jamaica. A survivor of domestic violence, from a previous marriage, suicidal tendencies, depression, huge financial debts and through the many challenges she has faced whilst parenting her son diagnosed with Special Needs, Michelle has taken the opportunity to turn her pain into a passion by sharing the experiences of her journey. Her insights and experience in life of overcoming difficulties has inspired many. Michelle strongly believes "your pain can become your passion" this passion has endowed her with abilities and strategies to help others overcome those stumbling blocks on their journey. She has spoken on stages alongside the likes of Tony Robbins.

The numerous challenges this inspirational woman has faced propelled her to not only write her books but to also assist others to share their story and has created coaching programs that has helped to change the life of others. Michelle strongly believes that '*your life is a book, you cannot go back and tear out the pages already written but you can determine what is going to be written in the next chapter of your book called life*' this passion has endowed her with the ability to share her thoughts, strategies and experiences to overcome those stumbling blocks and help you on your journey to success.

ACKNOWLEDGEMENTS

Firstly, I am ever thankful to God almighty as without Him nothing is possible. I am truly appreciative to the contributors – Martin Sharp, James Dewane, Leila Singh, Deenita Pattni, Claudia Crawley, Cheryl Chapman, Ben Green and Judith Wright. I would also like to take this time to thank one of my mentors Andy Harrington and His Professional Speakers Academy for all the knowledge and support I have received. Last but not least my family for being patient and supportive throughout the process and allowing me to live the dream of making an impact in the world.

Ben Green

I couldn't have asked for better support and experience than what has been given by Michelle to make my book idea possible and today I can now proudly hold my book in my hand and share its contents with the world.

Beata Bikowski

I cannot thank my amazing mentor Michelle Watson enough for not only helping me to publish my book but for also being an inspiration, for your belief in me and ongoing support, thank you.

John Foster

Michelle is amazing at what she does, from the mere idea of the book to becoming a published author. She continues to take an interest even after publishing as she remains in touch and takes the time to give further assistance where necessary. I would not hesitate to work with Michelle again in the future and I have recommended her to

other budding authors as I feel that she can bring out the best in them with her positive attitude and making them feel relaxed and confident so that they can produce their best work. Since the publication of the book I have become a speaker and run workshops based on my book for property Investors. I have also been asked by property investor groups to run further workshops and so my business has continued to grow since. The book has really helped my personal branding where I have become more visible and can be seen as an expert in my field.

Jennie Matthias

I feel very fortunate to have met Michelle and was so taken by her approach to assisting everyone that I immediately signed up for her Programme. It was affordable and worth every penny to now have my book in hand, a legacy that I will be able to leave behind. Michelle's approach to teaching is second to none, highly attentive and follows through after the event. Alongside my book I have created untold amounts of content under her guidance and with her guidance was able to host a phenomenal book launch.

Natalie Lawrence

Michelle has mentoring was one of the best things that has ever happened to me, her knowledge and expertise has supported me with rapid personal & business growth.

Michelle is an inspiration and what she has achieved given her challenges really inspired me to work with her. She is very friendly and supportive and having read her book and seen her talks found her drive and passion for what she does amazing and it comes across in everything that she does, with her help I now too have written and published my book".

Pete O'Keeffe

Michelle, you come from a place of abundance. What you teach to get a book published is gold. I wouldn't be published without your expertise

How's that!

Sandie Duggan

Michelle Watson is a true inspiration! An amazing mum, author, businesswoman and all round human being. A living example of the strength of the human spirit. Coming  back herself from adversity to shine her light and to help others on their journeys to be all that they can be. The fairy godmother of getting your book out there.... with a magic sprinkle of love, hope, wisdom and a kick up the butt when you need it!

Lightning Source UK Ltd.
Milton Keynes UK
UKHW040737051219
354823UK00002B/530/P

9 781999 620141